About the Author

Gavin Crosland is a Security Professional with a background in the British Special Forces. Over the past twenty years he has experimented with diet and exercise regimes designed to build a healthy and attractive body. Based on this experience he has effectively formulated a sustainable model for all to achieve their goals.

Dedications

Let us start by acknowledging all those who have contributed in some fashion to this book and ultimately made it happen. My thanks to you all:

Father Crosland – For sitting patiently through all those countless hours when, as a child, I demanded more and more Arnold Schwarzenegger films. And of course for providing me with my first set of weights all those years ago.

Erica – For putting up with a 'tubster' and seeing him back to normality with demands for a juicer.

Freddy – Your comment at the air show about my size in years to come hit me so much harder than anyone might have realised, and ultimately was a significant nail in the coffin.

Scott – A true friend, my gym constant, and my guru of sauna gossip.

Jason – My ambassador of blue, and mid-week 'carb hangover' sheriff.

Joe Cross – A truly inspirational man who has changed the lives of thousands across the globe.

Mirella Ingamells – A true subject matter expert who went to great lengths to support my requests and contribute to the content of this book…and who sports arguably the nicest bottom I've ever seen.

The Encore 10's – Who keep me motivated all year round!

Finally, my thanks to all the good sports who agreed to lend their names and photographs to this book. It wouldn't be the same without your stories.

Gavin Crosland

FROM FAT TO FANTASTIC

AUSTIN MACAULEY
PUBLISHERS LTD.

A CIP catalogue record for this title is available from the British Library.

ISBN 9781785542718 (Paperback)
ISBN 9781785542725 (Hardback)

www.austinmacauley.com

First Published (2015)
Austin Macauley Publishers Ltd.
25 Canada Square
Canary Wharf
London
E14 5LQ

Printed and bound in Great Britain

Contents

Introduction

Hello everyone and welcome to From Fat to Fantastic…your key to a new and better life! Hmmm, I almost feel as though that sentence should be read aloud in the style of a TV winter sale commercial – "It's fifty percent off and EVERYTHING MUST GO!" Well if we ever make a movie from this book then suffice to say we'll get a famous TV voiceover to read us in.

My congratulations to you for making the conscious decision to buy this book, well, hopefully or else it means I've been stiffed! In either event the important thing is you're here and presumably have made the decision to undertake a number of important changes in your life. If you've not fully committed as yet to that said decision, then keep on reading and we'll get you there. So on that note, let's get started…

To properly introduce myself, my name is Gavin, I'm thirty-six years old, and as of January 2014, I looked like this:

What can I say other than a picture paints a thousand words? And no, it really wasn't a pretty sight. I don't think you'll be shocked to learn that there weren't many modelling agencies fighting to sign me at that time!

Exactly four months on, despite continuing to eat all my favourite foods (chocolate, pizza, burgers, etc.), I looked like this:

Excuse the 'budgie smugglers,' I appreciate they're not everyone's cup of tea!

Note that these results were achieved without pills, potions, or any other fabled 'miracle cures.' Sadly these things don't exist, but more on that later. Obviously my results have come from time spent exercising, but more importantly as a result of my adopting a well-balanced, sustainable and much healthier diet. Oh, and whilst I still haven't been stopped on the street and offered my modelling contract, at least I have a better chance now!

The new diet I have adopted is **my version** of (what some refer to as) the 'hybrid diet.' Now I say the word 'diet' with utter contempt as this has the wrong connotations. Invariably when someone says they're going on a diet, it means they're going to cut back their food for a period of time to lose weight…only to then pack it all back on after the holiday or event where they needed to be able to squeeze in to that little black dress (or male equivalent, I don't want you to think I wear LBDs in my spare time!) When I refer to 'diet,' it's simply in the context of what we choose to eat on a regular basis. In this case, my diet is now subject to the '80-20 rule.' This means I eat healthily for the majority of my week and then let myself go at the weekend, allowing me a chance to eat all the 'bad foods' most of us crave. Eating healthily, for me, translates to juicing fresh fruits and vegetables, various smoothies, and eating natural unprocessed foods. We'll dive in to this in depth once we hit the chapter on Diet, but for now I simply want to offer you a brief insight into the very simple solutions that lay ahead in your future. And yes, they really are simple – just keep reading and trust me!

Of course the title of this book is really quite bold and it will be for you to decide if my transformation translates as 'fantastic.' Whether your answer is yes or otherwise, it really doesn't matter, the point is **I feel fantastic**. For many years I was embarrassed to take my top off in public. Whether you're fat, thin or any of the above, perhaps you know how that feels? Well, now I feel no shame and am the first up in the morning racing towards the pool.

Why am I writing this book? Well, the answer to that question is quite simple. Following my transformation I wrote a very short blog for a group promoting health & fitness who focused mostly on juicing diets. My intention was to demonstrate that I had been able to take aspects of their advice and apply it to my life in such a way that it would constitute a sustainable model – both in the short and long term. Having sent my blog to the group's administrator, it was subsequently posted on their website and Facebook page. Despite their only having a limited number of followers, I was amazed to see that within just a few hours it had received literally thousands of shares, likes and comments. I realised there was a strong appetite for others to learn more about my methods. Given that I'd only written a few paragraphs detailing how I achieved my transformation, there were naturally more questions to be answered; in fact I found myself inundated with questions on their pages and through people contacting me on social media forums. It occurred to me then that a far more detailed explanation was required, and here it is…

I certainly don't want you to be put off the thought of starting your own transformation by my statement that it took four months to achieve the results seen in my photographs. Yes, that is true but it is even more so based on the goal I set myself at that time, i.e. a four month countdown to my holiday (or vacation if you're reading this elsewhere in the world). I know from previous experience just how daunting it can be to stare down the barrel of several months of dieting and exercise. If you've attempted it before, then like me you may well have found you were good for a few weeks, saw little to no results, and then suddenly or gradually it all fell apart as you inevitably reverted back to your old bad habits. **The difference on this occasion was I immediately saw huge results. I quite literally lost 1.5 stone (9.5kg/21lb) within two weeks.** I instantly looked and felt better. Better still, everyone around me noticed and commented on my weight loss. This in turn inspired me to keep on going and work that much harder. Of course we'll track all the actions and results throughout the course of this book so that I can impart my success story to your good selves.

So, enough about me for the moment…what about you? Well, by the end of this book you'll successfully be armed with the following key information:

- We'll detail how to find the **real motivation** to make those all-important changes in your life, and most importantly, how to **stay motivated** after you've started to see results. You'll note that earlier I introduced my 'before (fat) pictures' as being taken in January 2014. This book has tracked my progress over the space of one year and offers honest feedback on my results. Whilst there has been some minor fluctuation in my physique, the good news is I've kept the weight off and am still looking and feeling great. Even better is that the initial changes I made in my life, particularly in my diet, now feel normal, as such I don't even have to think about them any more.

- We'll discuss the importance of avoiding 'diets' and instead how to effectively reboot your daily routines and achieve a sustainable lifestyle. Note that I used to hate the buzzword 'reboot' as it's used way too much. However, stick with me as it's about to become very close to your heart!

- We'll show you how to vastly improve your health, and thus live a longer and happier life. It's actually very possible to look great on the outside whilst being unhealthy on the inside. I know this from personal experience. Some of you may be suffering from health conditions. Amazing as it may sound, the changes you make by following my model may even serve to cure these.

- We'll offer better ways to exercise – both in and out of the gym. A wise man once said that if you're going to exercise then you have to do something you enjoy. There's no sense in my trying to force you into a gym if that's your personal idea of torture. Many of you will prefer to get your exercise on a sports field, riding a bike, playing a round of golf, or elsewhere - I'll leave it to you to add your own personal puns to the end of that one!

So my friends, let me conclude this introduction by saying that From Fat to Fantastic is not a gimmick. We're not sat here watching infomercials at 3am with models using rubber cables which promise to deliver quick and easy results – yeah right! **From Fat to Fantastic documents the past twenty years of my life experimenting with diet and exercise routines.** I intend to **consolidate** this knowledge into one simple guide and offer you the ability to eat delicious meals (**including all your favourite foods and snacks that you might have expected to be banned**) and if you choose to exercise, to **maximize your training regimes**. We'll do this without all the fluff, false promises and dreaded sales tactics.

Provided I've captured your attention, then let's get to it! Enjoy…

Chapter 1: Beware of False Promises

As you work your way through this book you'll notice that quite a few photos of me and my friends will appear. Why? Is this a result of my vanity? Hmmm, perhaps! No, not really. It's the old adage of the two people going for a job interview with the same qualifications, only one turns up in a suit whereas the other arrives wearing jeans and a t-shirt – who do you give the job to? Well, when I was a boy the message of the story was it was always the person in the suit. In today's society where Facebook and Google offices are decked out with pool tables and game stations this analogy might now be a bit out of date. However, you get the point. The same applies then to the message I'm selling in this book. If I was to join a new gym and hire a Personal Trainer, then I'd be inclined to choose the one with a body similar to the physique I want. That's logical, right? Well then, the key to these pictures is to show what can be achieved. I understand that on a personal level, I achieve the best results when inspired by others. Hopefully then, these visual aids will result in conveying the right message and metaphorically dressing me in the suit, whilst others come to you in their jeans!

I'll speak on motivation later, in depth. Finding my own motivation for this transformation came from an Australian guy called Joe Cross who, like me, had piled on a ton of weight, having abused his body for many years. Joe ultimately lost his weight by taking positive steps. We'll talk about Joe in depth during the next chapter. Whilst Joe and I have approached our transformations in slightly different fashions, the point for now is that Joe's story struck a real chord for me. I looked at him and found myself asking "If Joe can find his way back, then why can't I?" The answer was very simple and it was **YES**, I too could change my ways. Clearly now my intent is to do the same for you. Not to sound overly corny here but if I can help just one person reading this book to change their life, well then it's all been worth it.

Let's face it, if you've purchased a booked called 'From Fat to Fantastic' then there's a pretty fair chance that you're in the market to shift a few pounds. You very well may not want to look like me and that is fine; that will be controlled by the type of exercise you perform (if any) and we'll deal with that in a later section of the book. In fact, this book is intended to be quite broad so as to cater for people of all ages and abilities. Hey, you might be young with a great body now, but it's never too early to learn how to start eating a healthier diet. Perhaps you're in shape and are looking for new tips on how to push your workouts to the next level? Have you a high metabolism and can't put on weight? Do you need to take the same journey as me and lose all that chub? Well you're all very welcome and will be catered for here.

The ultimate purpose of this book is to offer you a single, consolidated guide that will serve to sustain your training and dietary requirements for the rest of your life.

For most of my adult life, I was very serious about my physique and invested literally thousands of hours into exercising so I could look good. As I got older a number of changes that had occurred in my life led to a quite massive weight gain. Over the decades I've read countless articles on health and fitness from respected sources. Most recently, during my fat years, I was sent numerous diet plans by friends. With so many options on the market for losing weight and getting in shape, what's the real answer? I know from personal experience that I experimented with a number of different routines and diets which promised to deliver results, however none did.

Ask yourself this simple question: 'How has the Health and Fitness industry become a multi-billion dollar global phenomenon?' Now I can understand spending money at gyms and on home gym equipment – that's fine, this offers us the ability to exercise, which is very important. But what about these companies who are able to keep selling their fitness magazines on a monthly basis? Why are Personal Trainers continuously attending seminars to learn the latest trends in diet and exercise? Is the human body really evolving that fast or are we literally making astonishing breakthroughs on a monthly basis that will revolutionise the way we achieve the ultimate six-pack and live in the utopia of optimum health? ABSOLUTELY NOT! This industry needs to keep us all coming back time and time again as they're in it for the money. It's as simple as that. A high percentage of courses people attend will be considered obsolete within the coming years, otherwise how are the 'experts' to sell their new exercise discoveries, diet fads or much worse, fabled miracle cures? Sure, I agree we are constantly learning and that serious improvements have been made over the decades, and I'm positive that breakthroughs will continue to be made over the decades to come. However the basic principles continue to apply – work hard, eat well…and you'll achieve your goals. It's just that simple! Everything you need to look and feel healthy is contained within this book. If, later, you want to take it to the next level and start competing in bodybuilding competitions on stage, well then you'll need to move on to another book as we're not covering that subject here. You might be surprised to learn that those people walking on stage for said competitions are far from being at their peak health levels, they're actually dangerously dehydrated and that's just for starters! Again, here we're focused on looking good, but far more importantly, being healthy.

As this book is centred on being open, honest and focusing on what actually does work, let me offer you a prime example about how people can be fooled by myths and gimmicks. Unfortunately not all transformations are successful and not all messages out there are quite as positive as the one being pushed by Joe Cross. We'll start with a real life example which is quite a sad story. Some years ago I had a friend; for the sake of anonymity we'll call him John. John was a normal guy with a normal job and a normal body. In his early thirties he decided he wasn't happy and wanted to make a change in his physique and career, and as such John decided to become a Personal Trainer. To his credit, John threw himself into this lifestyle change with such commitment and enthusiasm that we all became inspired. The sad thing though was that John became all-consumed by his new industry and forgot how to enjoy it – he was one of those people who would turn up to a dinner party or a wedding with his own food because he was determined to achieve his goal of the perfect body. A tad extreme? I'd say so! I've heard lots of these examples, such as people eating their roast dinner on a Sunday and then waiting to have their roast potatoes four hours later to maximize the benefits of how their body processes the food. Seriously, what has the world come to? Anyway, back to John...

John spent tens of thousands of pounds on health and fitness related courses in the space of a few years. He was fooled into believing that in order to be fully qualified to sell his services, he had to be current with the latest trends and techniques. Whilst I can appreciate a degree of logic here, I think you'll understand my point when I tell you that John soon racked up a debt of £50,000. Whoops! It will take a seriously long time to see a return on that investment! Please remember, whatever level you're going in at, there are endless numbers of companies out there waiting to get their hands on your money. John would blindly follow every new piece of information that came his way from so called 'experts.' Unfortunately I can't remember the precise detail of this part of the story, however there was a time when John was promoting the benefit of a new drug on the market to our group of friends. He was convinced this was the best thing since sliced bread and believed in it wholeheartedly, as it had come from a study conducted by a doctor. We didn't think his information sounded overly convincing so we Googled the name of the doctor. If I recall correctly the first page of Google results was dedicated to this doctor being linked to various scandals and naming him as a scam artist. We reported this back to John, who amazingly refused to acknowledge our discovery and continued to back the product! If this doesn't serve as a cautionary tale of how one can be entirely bewildered then nothing will...

The saddest part of John's story is that despite all his effort and financial investment, he never achieved the body he wanted. Let's face it, if you're reading this and/or pursuing a career in fitness, then that's really what we're all here for. John struggled to get his weight down and went through some truly odd diets in his attempts. I remember on one occasion asking him what he was having for dinner that night. John told me he was boiling up (if I remember correctly) some vegetables and fish and was going to drink the juices – he wasn't going to eat the fish and veggies, only drink the juice! When telling me this, his expression seemed to me a combination of depression and hopefulness as he uttered the words "I'm hoping it will boil and form a broth." There you go, you can both follow my regime and eat delicious, healthy food (and your favourite naughty foods for two days of the week), or you can starve yourself, take your own food to parties and drink broth for dinner. Hopefully this should be an easy choice for you to make!

John and I rarely agreed on diet, in fact we out-and-out argued on the subject. John's justification was based on the number of courses he had attended (as we've discussed, at extreme personal financial expense). My argument on the other hand was as such:

1. He'd been in the industry for a very short space of time; I had been following fitness trends for twenty years.

2. I'd personally experimented with diet for many years and discovered first-hand what does and doesn't work. This includes having trained myself and helping others to achieve the bodies of their dreams.

3. By the time John had turned to the world of fitness I had already put on vast amounts of weight. John couldn't see past my being fat, despite my having shown him photos of me when I was younger and in much better shape than him. Surely if you can demonstrate your point with physical evidence then that should be the end of the argument? Sadly that wasn't enough for John.

John also subscribed to the theory of high protein diets. This is very common if you speak to Personal Trainers. It's great if your aim is to develop muscle, however if you're trying to lose weight then it's really not the best way to go – at least not until you've first lost the weight. I personally don't believe that fuelling your body with such high doses of protein is terribly healthy, certainly not in the long term. A short time ago (the summer of 2014) the latest report being pushed by doctors was that more than two servings of red meat per week puts you at an increased risk of developing cancer. Well, I don't know if that is true, as such reports seem to invariably contradict themselves within a space of a few years; however it does at least fit the model of moderating the food you eat. I do entirely subscribe to the need for a life of **moderation**. Moderation is the key to a sustainable future for us all.

The last time I saw John he had given up on getting his weight down as he was convinced he didn't have a body type that allowed him to achieve a lean physique. Actually, John had been close, but the effort needed was so high that it led to depression. Instead he convinced himself that he should pursue new goals according to what his 'alleged' body type could actually achieve. I believe John then started down the power lifting path and became very big and heavy with muscle. Hey, it's fine if you like that kind of thing but it's a far cry from what he originally entered the fitness game to do. I firmly believe this to be a case of 'Cognitive Dissonance.' If you're not familiar with this term then a basic explanation is to say that your mind can't deal with conflicting attitudes or beliefs. A good example would be Nazis at the concentration camps in the Second World War. It wouldn't be possible to commit such atrocities (even under orders) if you didn't condition your mind to accept you were doing the right thing. In John's case he spent years feeling unhappy with his body, only to then change his opinions and fully embrace a new path. I agree you shouldn't become obsessed with certain results and should remain flexible; but it's unfortunate to see how he completely changed his goals due to tackling the issue without good information.

Sadly, all John really needed was a juicer and it might have all been different. It's very sad story, yet let's take the positive from this as an important cautionary tale for others.

Of course, you don't have to follow John's extreme route to be caught up in all the other false promises out there. Have you ever spotted an advertisement on the internet offering you the diet pill that has revolutionised the market? How about the new training supplement that will give you the muscles of your dreams? Well if you haven't seen these then you've been living under a rock! Trust me when I say I've taken many diet pills available on the public market (i.e. without the need for a doctor's prescription) over the years and have NEVER seen any results from these. **<u>NEVER</u>**. That is to say I've taken them whilst training and eating well…in which case I was losing weight anyway. I've also taken them whilst not in training and not eating the right foods, and unsurprisingly they had zero effect. Please, please, **PLEASE**, do not waste your hard-earned money on these, it's just nonsense. There is no substitute for good old fashioned hard work and moderation.

So we've briefly discussed the ads for pills and potions (a brief paragraph is all they deserve), but what about the promises made by companies selling their latest home exercise equipment and/or training DVDs? Again, I'm sure we've all seen plenty of these examples over the years – the classic 3am infomercials. The obvious example is the infamous 'Thigh Master' which you could use in various exercises all over your body to 'get ripped.' As always, they were being used by smiling models in great shape, without so much as a bead of sweat on their body or a hair out of place. Now if you want to try these out then by all means, go ahead – it's all exercise at the end of the day which is not going to do you any harm. However, don't expect these gadgets sold at $59.99 over the phone to deliver the same results being sported by those smiling models. More likely, expect it to be used for a short period and then stuffed in your garage as you tuck into yet another tub of ice cream.

The best home exercise product I've seen is Shaun T's Insanity programme. If you haven't seen this before then look it up as this guy does know what he's talking about and really will deliver the results he's promising. In addition you can buy in to his support package with trainers tracking your progress and offering you encouragement. Of course you can order his nutritional supplements to assist in fuelling your workouts; Shaun T is clearly not going to miss out on an opportunity to maximize his profits. Now, I don't believe you need to buy in to the supplements part, as you can get everything you need by eating the right foods. Yes, you'll see in the Diet Chapter of this book that I do use protein supplements (linked to my training regimen), but these are very basic level products and readily available in your local supermarket – there's really no need to buy in to any special programmes. Of course this is my opinion only and I can't speak as an authority on Shaun T's nutritional supplements (no one wants to be sued here!)

Shaun T's message is fantastic in that he doesn't claim to be able to make you look like him. I might suggest you Google images of Shaun T so that you can fully appreciate what I mean. What he does promise is to get you in the best possible shape. I like that message as it's impossible to aim to look like anyone else; you can only hope to achieve the best results possible in your own body.

However, as with all the other providers out there, even Shaun T's promises are not without an element of fiction. He has multiple products on the market; I've come across Insanity and Hip Hop Abs but there are probably more. Both promise to deliver high results whilst working at very different ends of the spectrum – Insanity is basically hardcore circuit training and Hip Hop Abs is designed as a way to 'dance yourself thin.' Now don't get me wrong, I've seen both and they're both excellent, I own Insanity and have used it at home on many occasions as part of my training regime. However (there's always a however with these things!), don't believe you're going to dance around your living room and end up with pecs or biceps like Shaun T, it's just not going to happen without some serious time spent pumping iron in the gym. This also applies to Insanity. If done right that will deliver a lean, toned body and you will develop muscle, however not to the extent of Shaun T. It's all a case of understanding how exercise will affect your body differently. To be completely fair to Shaun T, he too acknowledges that if you want to build muscle then you do have to spend some time lifting weights. He also sells an extended DVD set which offers a glimpse of this side of his training programme.

Some of you reading this book might be surprised that I am promoting Shaun T's products and encouraging you to take a look at his website. Well let's be very clear now that From Fat to Fantastic is not claiming to be the reinvention of the wheel. It is my aim to deliver information to you on what really does work and effectively consolidate, in one book, the best practices spread out there through many sources. I do believe in the mantra that 'you never stop learning'. Whilst I certainly have made a lot of useful discoveries first-hand which are to be shared here; a great deal of my knowledge has come from others whom I've either met over the years, or like the Shaun T's of the world, have seen on screen or read about.

So, let's summarise this section…

If you're serious about changing the way you look then unfortunately there is no miracle cure out there. So on that note, don't buy in to any more of these false promises. Some of you might be screaming 'gastric bypass' as you read this and if that's your answer to the miracle cure question, well then you're welcome to it! Before you decide on taking that route I do suggest you first look into the negative side effects of such a procedure. Back to reality - there just is no substitute for good old-fashioned blood, sweat and tears. If you want it, then you'll have to work for it. This statement applies to both your new diet, and if you decide to exercise, then in your new training regime. You'll notice I constantly refer to your ability to choose to exercise. Well let's cut through that and now just take it as a given that you may or may not want to exercise – I suggest you do, if nothing else then for your own health, but that's your choice. Even if you only choose to follow the diet plans set out in this book then you're still going to see results in your body and vastly improve your health.

So if there is no miracle cure and we're going to have to work for our results, then it means there's a tough road ahead. However (there's that however again), the great news is we're going to tackle said road by applying the rule of 'moderation.' The road only has to be as hard as you choose to make it. This book isn't Shaun T's Insanity (anyone who's tried that workout will tell you it lives up to its name!), this is your essential guide to choosing how hard you want to work and how to make these new steps last for the rest of your life.

Chapter 2: Knowledge is Power

Growing up in the 80's, I was privy to the era of Sylvester Stallone and Jean-Claude Van Damme style action movies, i.e. big, muscular bodies that were all the rage. From an early age, Arnold Schwarzenegger became my hero and I developed an interest in bodybuilding. Whilst I successfully parlayed that intrigue into many a gruelling hour in gyms, I never went down the route of the quintessential bodybuilder type – don't worry, it's not that kind of book! When I was sixteen I started out with a push-up and sit-up routine I devised at home. I gradually moved my way on to gyms as I learned more about the most effective ways to train. A few years later I found myself in the British Army, initially serving as a member of the Royal Military Police, but ending my service in a branch of the British Special Forces. Obviously my knowledge of how best to exercise increased exponentially during those years. You might find it interesting to learn that exercise doesn't necessarily guarantee you the body of your dreams, certainly 90% of the soldiers I knew really didn't look great at all and there were countless occasions where I was asked by them to either write their training programmes and/or train them so they could achieve their goal of the hallowed six pack. There's no great secret here, these people simply weren't training in the right way to achieve sculpted muscle and more importantly, their diets were just all wrong.

As promised, we'll keep on pulling in a few photos to demonstrate the statements being made:

Yes, based on these photos I arguably watched too many 80's movies!

Being young, attractive and of course, a lethal weapon (eat your heart out Mel Gibson!) I had no idea that within the space of a few short years, I'd make this transformation:

During my teens and twenties I remained quite dedicated to maintaining a good physique. Yes, I of course had periods in my life where I couldn't find the motivation to get off my bed and hit the gym. **Part of preparing yourself for your own journey is accepting the fact that you can't stay in peak condition all year round** – those who can are a very rare breed. More importantly, for the sake of this book, I also spent those years experimenting with my diet. When I was young I foolishly thought the key to a healthy and attractive body was eating very little. I'd effectively starve myself, only eating fruit, drinking milk (which I thought was the key to my protein intake), eating very basic salads and limited meat. What a fool I was! I learned this the hard way, i.e. I effectively starved myself between the ages of sixteen to seventeen thinking it was the best way to stay thin. Thankfully I then went on holiday in Tenerife with a friend (my first 'lad's holiday'). For a week we ate like normal people and I stuffed myself every morning with a Full English Breakfast (lots of meat and eggs for those who don't know what that is). The results were amazing in that I finally gave my muscles the fuel they were craving and within a week I filled out and looked 100% better. We'll discuss the importance of fuelling your body properly later in this book.

Just so we're clear, you can't stuff yourself constantly with bacon, sausage and eggs and expect it not to eventually put a few pounds around your waist in addition to fuelling your muscles! Remember, moderation is the key.

Another prime example of where I went wrong at one stage was in an attempt to cut all 'bad foods' from my life. So that meant no pizza, chocolate, bread, or our other favourite processed foods. The result? Well, I'd manage to keep it up for a while, though inevitably I'd fall off the wagon and gorge myself on all the things I'd been missing. Once that started, I'd not be able to stop as the thought of going without my favourite foods would act as a major road block to 'eating clean' again. This, in turn, would affect my attitude towards exercise - if I wasn't eating the right diet, then what was the point of going to the gym? That was a disastrous position to find myself in and so pledging to never eat chocolate again was totally counterproductive. Invariably it would take me a couple of months and lots of weight gain to eventually say enough was enough and get back to the gym. Ultimately I found the answer to be - that's right, you've probably guessed it - moderation. It's all about the 80-20 rule.

When I turned thirty I found it was getting harder to keep the body I had in my twenties. I simply chalked that one up to my getting older and my body changing. My waist size was increasing but hey, that's what happens when you get older, right? Well yes, that may eventually be the case, but not this early on. In case you doubt this statement then let me tell you I'm now wearing 32'' trousers again; this is something I haven't done since I was twenty-two years old. It really is true that you never stop learning. Whilst in my twenties I was quietly smug that I was the authority on exercise and achieving a sexy body, but it just goes to prove that I still didn't have it quite right.

As I got older it became harder to see the definition in my abs, however this was the least of my troubles and it was all about to change dramatically. Age thirty was the turning point for me. By that stage I'd been out of the Army for five years and although I'd managed to keep up my exercise routine, I'd become truly bored of all those hours spent in the gym. The more prevalent factor was that my life had changed dramatically. I'd found myself in a very comfortable relationship and I was in a new job that didn't afford me the time to train or eat healthily. Suddenly I had new priorities at home and at work that superseded my vanity. So it was goodbye to the gym and hello to being wined & dined on business class flights and at 'power lunches.' It doesn't take a fortune teller to predict the outcome of this new routine. Yes, within a very short space of time I'd packed on the blubber, gaining a total of 2 stone (15kg/33lb). I'll be honest and tell you that I put on a very brave outward face to the world as though I didn't care, however at night I'd lie in bed fantasising about having my old body back. Being fat and unattractive depressed me deeply. Now I appreciate, of course, that these days we all live in a very politically correct world and you can't say that being fat equates to being unattractive as you may risk hurting someone's feelings. Well that may actually be true in some cases...but for me, I looked **<u>awful!</u>** Suffice to say I wasn't being approached by any attractive ladies in bars offering to buy me a drink! That may not be what drives you in life, but for me it did affect the way I felt about myself.

So, in a short space of time I packed on the pounds and this happened:

By this stage it's still apparent that there was a time in my life when I was muscular...but also clear that I'd had way too many nights attacking the cookie jar. And yes, I'm definitely holding in my stomach in this photo!

As I alluded to earlier, I did on occasion make attempts to lose the weight. I'd apply all the lessons I'd learned in the past and where possible, would exercise as much as I could. Sadly the results would come so slowly and would involve so much effort that I'd quickly give up. My most successful stint involved me carrying natural nuts (unsalted and uncooked) and a bag of carrots around the world on my business trips so that I wouldn't be tempted by the minibars in hotels...believe me, carrying and eating these soon gets pretty boring! It's also embarrassing being sat on a plane declining your meal from the cabin crew whilst scoffing a carrot with a miserable look on your face! Now I appreciate not all readers of this book will have experienced the same lifestyle I'm describing, but I'm sure most of you can equate your own experiences to mine in one form or another. Too busy at work to get to the gym or eat a decent meal? Eating late at night because you've had a long day and you didn't get a chance to earlier? You're a mother nibbling at the kids' food during feeding time? Sure, I could have a salad…but McDonalds is right next door and I could murder a Quarter Pounder! Oh yes, the list is endless!

Before I knew it, six long years had passed. I'd thrown out my old wardrobe and gradually replaced it for a new one that fitted. Yes, it was depressing having to buy ever bigger clothes and admitting to myself that yet again my trousers were getting tight and I needed ones with a larger waist.

Depending on where you are in your own journeys, some of you may not think I looked too bad. If we compare the before and after pictures throughout, then hopefully this should support my message. I trialled this recently on a couple of friends, their disgusted expressions seemed to support my theory that before I was an utter porker! Let's try this one:

Believe me; the second version of me feels an awful lot better in every possible way!

I have to confess that it's quite a struggle finding suitable photos to add to this book from my fat days. I was so unhappy with my appearance that I really didn't have many photos taken of me, certainly not with my top off. On some level I think we don't like to be reminded of how bad we look when we've let ourselves go a bit – perhaps you'll agree? A month before I began my transformation I found myself on holiday with my family. We spent a lot of time on the beach where lots of photos were taken. Halfway through the holiday I saw some of the pictures and realised just how bad I really looked. Somehow in my mind I'd built up a defensive wall and convinced myself I'd lost weight and didn't look too bad. When I saw the photos, however, I didn't want to go back to the beach and although I put on a brave face, it actually spoiled the rest of the trip for me.

Right then, enough looking back at the past and feeling sorry for myself. Let's move on and discuss where it all changed…

Around the time I went on that fateful family trip, it had been suggested I buy a juicer – not a blender or a smoothie maker, but a juicer designed to extract the fluid from vegetables and fruit. I admit I was sceptical. I'd heard of others buying these and thought it was just another fad and yet another gadget that would soon be resigned to my cupboard together with my bread maker (which seemed a good idea at the time!) Meanwhile, with the juicer in the cupboard, I'd be financially out of pocket and still wolfing down chocolate brownies as normal. Again, I'm always sceptical of any of these diets or fads. Does anyone remember 'Eat for Your Type?' This was a book written by a doctor that said you should eat certain foods according to your blood type. Based on the theory of how mankind has evolved it set out all the foods you should eat, right down to the type of fruits you are allowed (according to the book I wasn't allowed any citrus fruits, and that was the tip of the iceberg). I remember this being very popular for about five minutes until mostly everyone got bored and went back to their normal routines. I'm sure you're all aware of other examples you've been exposed to. There are some popular companies out there who help you lose weight by attending their group sessions to talk about weight loss and track your progress. To me this seems like a lot of wasted time you could have spent exercising and actually doing something about your weight problem! Also they tend to sell their own ranges of food which you're encouraged to buy in to. If you've seen the portion sizes of these then it's no wonder you lose weight – they're tiny! Also the food they offer is pretty tasteless, offers you limited options for variety and is an expensive way to eat. All in all it strikes me as a whole lot of wasted effort that could be put to much better use in more positive areas.

Despite my reservations, I agreed to buy a juicer and at least give it a try.

Before my juicer arrived I was flicking my way through Netflix and stumbled across a documentary by Joe Cross (whom I mentioned earlier) called 'Fat, Sick and Nearly Dead.' A bit of an extreme title? Well, I thought so. However from the cover I could see it was a film centred on juicing so I said "What the hell, it's got to be worth a try"

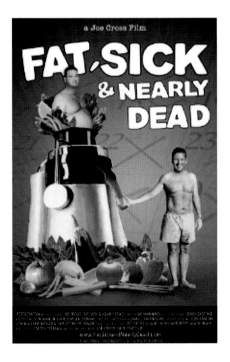

Again, I will be totally honest - I was a sceptic. After all, I don't normally buy in to all this 'mumbo jumbo!' I'd previously watched 'Supersize Me' and despite its obvious and clear message, having stared at Big Macs for ninety minutes I was desperate for a McDonald's! Perhaps it was unclear to some but surely anyone with half a brain cell would know that eating nothing but junk food would be seriously detrimental to their health? So, was 'Fat, Sick and Nearly Dead' to be yet another documentary stating nothing but the obvious? Well with a juicer in the mail I decided it was worth at least a quick look…

What I found in Fat, Sick and Nearly Dead was a highly informative and highly inspirational documentary. You can find the film on Netflix, can rent it on YouTube, or can buy the DVD. I strongly recommend watching this one. I've personally watched it many times and have even used it to re-motivate myself when I've felt myself reaching for the takeaway menus. A prime example of this occurred when I was several months into my transformation. I had to travel to Brussels for a business meeting. I arrived late the night before and checked in to my hotel. Too tired to hit the gym and too grumpy to have something healthy, I ordered myself a burger and fries from room service, with a chocolate dessert to follow. The following morning I felt a bit lethargic and decided not to bother with the gym. Then for some reason I decided to put on Fat, Sick and Nearly Dead…ten minutes later I'd pulled out a juice from the mini-bar (which I'd brought from home) and started banging out push-ups in the room. Thanks for keeping me faithful, Joe!

Fat, Sick and Nearly Dead essentially charts the transformations of Joe and a guy he meets on his travels in the United States, namely, Phil. Phil is the stereotypical obese American. The change Phil inevitably makes in his life is really quite touching. However it was Joe's story that really caught my attention. He introduced the movie by explaining how he'd previously been healthy and active, but then life had got in the way – basically his priorities were focused on everything but his health and he had a natural love for processed foods such as pizza and fizzy drinks. Cut then to a scene with Joe at the pool sporting a huge belly. And that was it, I was hooked! Why? Because I saw myself in Joe and said "This guy is living my life!"

I've tried to offer you, the reader, some of my personal story as perhaps you might be able to relate some of your own experiences to mine. If you can do this then it will hopefully put you in a better frame of mind when starting your own journey.

As you would expect, Joe and Phil both lost a ton of weight, an achievement in itself. However, the film went much further than that. Both Joe and Phil were suffering from the same rare skin condition which is a form of chronic hives and resulted in their both having to take high levels of medication to combat the condition on a daily basis. Joe made the point that our bodies have the ability to heal themselves – if you scrape your knee then your body, in time, will repair the broken skin. So why couldn't his body cure his condition? Joe's theory then was if he fuelled his body with all the nutrients required then his body could recover. And that he did! Both he and Phil eventually came off their medication and stopped suffering from hives.

Joe and Phil are not the only examples I have heard of about curing skin conditions through juicing. Some of you may have heard of Jason Vale, another chap considered to be a guru in the world of juicing…if you haven't come across him then get back on Google and look him up. By the end of 2014 I found myself dating a nutritionist – I suppose not such an odd coincidence considering my new interest in this area. Her name is Louise. As I have said, you never stop learning. I was able to glean many new insights from Louise. Her nutritional advice and programmes are much the same as mine. They centre on juicing and healthy eating. She'd spent a lot of time working with Jason Vale and was (I'm informed), included as part of his advertisements and promotional packs. Whilst Louise had trained in her younger years, when I met her she hadn't exercised for eighteen months due to a spinal injury. However, despite not exercising for a long period and having had two children, Louise still sported an incredible body and amazingly, her stomach was firmer than mine! So, two children on and in her early thirties, this is what Louise looks like:

If that's not a body ready for the beach then I don't know what is!

I've spoken with plenty of mothers over the years that have claimed their bodies have changed as a result of their pregnancy and they can't lose weight as a result. Louise is a clear example that you don't need to turn to the extreme routes of surgery to drop that baby weight. No more excuses, there is a way back for everyone!

Back to Jason Vale. Louise told me how, as with Joe and Phil, Jason had also suffered with a chronic skin condition. He then embarked on a ninety day detox (drinking only natural vegetable and fruit juice) until he eventually cured himself of this condition. I find this amazing. For me it further demonstrates just what our bodies can do when properly fuelled.

Also, back to Joe Cross – I feel like a comedian cutting back and forth between stories to cleverly link them all for the end punch line! As I've said, Fat, Sick and Nearly Dead had me hooked in every aspect. Yes, I was amazed by the weight loss and yes, I was fascinated by the natural cures to health problems. However even more so than this, Joe forced me to take a very stark look at my own life in ways I couldn't have imagined before. Although not as extreme as the likes of Joe or Jason Vale, I too was suffering from the symptoms of being overweight and unhealthy. I felt tired and lethargic; I'd developed dry skin on my back, and as a result of the added weight was starting to struggle with my ankles and knees. It's quite hard on your joints to carry around all that blubber. So what was Joe's point that captivated me so? Well, it was his explanation on what actually constitutes a healthy diet. Of course I knew that when I became fat it was as a result of the choices I'd made and was my fault. It wasn't as though someone was sneaking in to my kitchen at night and injecting my celery with millions of calories! However, when I was younger (and training) I considered my diet to be well balanced and healthy…how wrong I was.

If you're reading this book elsewhere in the world then this might not apply, however a typical dinner in the West will consist of fifty percent protein (your meat), twenty-five percent carbohydrates (your potato) and only twenty-five percent vegetables. It's the vegetables that deliver those all-important macronutrients that our bodies need. Worst of all for me, the times when I would eat raw vegetables – when they are in their best state – was almost non-existent.

I'm not going to become overly embroiled in the science side of foods in this book; after all I am not qualified as a doctor or nutritionist. If you yourself want to become an expert on the science of food then there is plenty of data available out there and you can have a chat with your own doctor. What I will quote are the best practices generally accepted as 'common knowledge.' This essentially translates to…that's right, you guessed it, everything in moderation and the importance of eating enough fruit and vegetables. Of course, what is enough? The majority of doctors in the West typically recommend consuming five daily servings of fruits and vegetables. Of course, as with most medical advice it all seems to change on a semi-regular basis. I've lost track of how many news reports I've heard informing us that some certain foods will give us cancer, the following week we'll be told the same foods are good for us. It seems now however (according to a recent BBC News report I watched), that Western doctors are recommending seven servings of fruits and vegetables per day. But what about other areas of the world? I'm of the understanding that Japanese doctors stipulate seventeen servings of fruits and vegetables per day. Seriously?! HOW?!!! Fortunately these days I actually do tend to get that many on a regular basis…through the medium of juicing. As to the Japanese, whilst this guidance does at first glance appear to be, now what's the right word for it? Oh that's it – **MENTAL** – perhaps they're actually on to something? Reports suggest that within the not too distant future the Japanese economy shall no longer be able to sustain pension funds, essentially as there are just so many elderly people refusing to kick the bucket. Hmmm, pass me the spinach, Sir!

Now I realise we all like to poke fun at the concept of our own mortality, claiming "when it's my time, then it's my time." However, if you've ever had a true medical scare during your life where you believe yourself to be staring down the barrel of an imminent departure, you'll know just how false that statement really is. I want to live and I want to live well! I realise of course that it's the decisions I make now that will ultimately affect me later in life. I've seen far too many cases of late in my work colleagues – whom all enjoyed extended periods of over-indulgence – who are now suffering from strokes, cancer, and other life changing illnesses from their fifties onwards. Come on, that's just too soon – agreed? So, based on this premise It dawned on me that if I didn't make a permanent change now, in another twenty years or so I'll be facing the same health issues I'm starting to see in my family and business colleagues. Cancer, diabetes, strokes, and so on. I question how many cases could have been avoided by living a healthier lifestyle?

I was so inspired by Joe's message that I began to follow his advice with my juicer. As the weight started to fall off me, my friends and family all started asking me for my secret. "Watch Fat, Sick and Nearly Dead" I'd always say. I've continued to follow Joe and his company, Reboot With Joe, for some time, including meeting him in London for the screening of Fat, Sick and Nearly Dead 2. What a thoroughly nice chap he is too:

Another amazing by-product of Fat, Sick and Nearly Dead was that it inspired me to do better with my health in other areas of my life. Yes, I took on the concept of juicing. So long as I was doing the diet piece I decided I may as well get back in the gym. As the weight started falling off me I was duly inspired to work harder in the gym to see faster and better results. As I became further interested in my health, I was even able to finally quit smoking, something I'd tried to do on countless occasions in the past. The point I'm making is I started making those little changes in my health, ultimately it led me much further than I'd expected.

So the obvious question at this stage might be "If all the answers are there in Fat, Sick and Nearly Dead, why do we need to read this book?" Ah ha, good question! Well the answer is simple. As with every other piece of information I've come across in my life on the subject of health and fitness, I've extracted the best bits and adapted it to a format that suits my own life. This is the key for us all – even if you don't follow my routine to the letter, find a way to take the best bits and make it work for you.

In Fat, Sick and Nearly Dead, Joe essentially embarked on a detox whereby he had only juice for a full sixty days. Again let me clarify, that's not that awful stuff you find in your local supermarket, the juice came from passing raw fruits and vegetables through a juicer. I now won't drink purchased fruit juices at all as I can't bear the thought of what has been added. Joe also committed that after his fast he would eat only fruits and vegetables until his skin condition was cured…and he did it. Well done Joe!

I, on the other hand, had no intention of fasting for sixty days straight. Joe also suggests that people try a ten day fast (detox). In my mind, both are merely temporary solutions and are not sustainable. Yes, I could complete either version but like all other crazy diet fads, I knew there would come a time where I would simply fall off the wagon and never go back to 'punishing' myself by only drinking juice for a period of time. I said to myself I wanted to incorporate Joe's teachings into my own life in such a way that I could keep it up indefinitely, thus managing my weight and health levels all in one fell swoop. And this is exactly what I did. In the Diet Chapter of this book I'll guide you through my process and demonstrate, step by step, the results it offered.

When I attended the Screening of Fat, Sick and Nearly Dead 2, Joe was very open in telling us all that his weight has fluctuated since we last saw him in the first film – if I remember correctly it was within the region of 20lbs here and there. Also there was a very sad story to be heard in that Phil (the obese American guy who lost hundreds of pounds), had gone back to his old ways and put the weight back on again. Both Joe and Phil attributed the weight fluctuations to various factors such as work schedules, managing routines and stress, amongst others. For the most part Joe has managed to keep all his weight off (I suppose this is his business so he has an added incentive that most of us don't). Phil, on the other hand, had met a new woman, fallen head over heels for her and very quickly got married. When the marriage soon failed it pushed him over the edge and that was his catalyst for putting down the juicer and heading back to the fast food outlets. Yes, it was very sad indeed, but for me, served as further evidence that we all must find our own natural rhythm and learn to live within **moderation**. No more crazy diets that don't last **please!**

Like Joe and Phil, since starting my journey I have had quite a year. My job continues to be very demanding with sixty plus hour weeks. Sadly my marriage failed and I'm now in the process of getting divorced. I have financial stresses linked to my divorce, and I'm having to move home again – I believe they say moving home is about the most stressful thing you can do, I would be inclined to wholeheartedly agree! **However**, having not set myself any crazy routines I'm still able to follow my **normal** diet plan. I can still do this as quite frankly, it's easy. Also I can still eat the 'comfort food' I'm craving now (linked to all of my recent life stresses) as it was always part of my diet plan. It's very hard to fall off the wagon when you've not given up on 'the wrong food groups' in the first place. So a year on I've just returned from a holiday and here's how I look:

So you can see that one year on, despite all the life stresses, I've managed to keep the weight off. The holiday was very much an impromptu affair, i.e. I decided to go and one week later I was on the plane – thus I had no time to change my diet and train differently. I'm not in as good shape as I was when I reached the four month point of my transformation (as seen in the Introduction to this book), however I'm not currently aiming towards any specific goals (we'll deal with this in the Get Motivated Chapter of this book). For now I'm simply in a 'maintenance mode' and am happy with how I look. Feeling happy with yourself and being healthy is the ultimate goal, to hell with what anyone else thinks. And remember, how I look now is still a far cry from this beast:

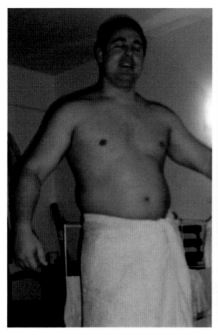 

Okay, I think that should just about cover my background story. Now that you understand what led me to become a porker and equally how I was inspired to bring myself back, let's now move forward and focus on your transformations.

Chapter 3: Get Motivated

If you're anything like me, you might have skimmed your way through the previous chapters screaming "I don't care! I didn't buy this book to read about how and why you got fat, just tell me what **I** need to do to change!" That's absolutely fine, that section will mean more to some than everyone reading this book. **However, this chapter is not one to be skipped. This is arguably the most important chapter of the entire book.** Take your time to read this section and consider how it applies to your own life.

If I had a pound for every time I'd said "I'm sick of looking like this, the diet starts on Monday" then I'd be a rich man by now. I've lost count of the number of times I promised myself and everyone around me that I was going to get back in shape. As always, it just never happened. It's true that I was sick of looking and feeling bad, however my best intentions to begin was always stalled by the following -

1. I knew how much hard work lay ahead and how long it would take achieve the goals I had set for myself.

and

2. I hadn't conditioned my mind in such a way that I felt **I must change**.

We're all different and are all inspired in different ways. As such I can't realistically hope to tell you how to become motivated. You're going to have to decide that for yourself based on what drives you. I can, however, offer you an explanation of my triggers that finally got me going again and offer ideas of the thought process you should take.

Without your motivation in place, the chances of you succeeding in your quest are very low. So start planning!

At a personal level, I was always motivated as a younger man to exercise because it made my body look good. A sexy body gives you a better shot at getting a sexy lady…well, it's not going to hurt your chances at the very least! I was married to a lovely woman for seven years who didn't mind that I'd put on weight. Suddenly the key to my motivation had been removed. So how do you get it back? Ditch the wife? Well that's a tad extreme! I'm pleased to say my weight loss had nothing to do with the end of my marriage – not that it matters for the sake of this book but we simply grew apart and remain good friends to this day.

For years I'd been going on an annual holiday with a group of friends. Not everyone in this group could afford to go to some of the places around the world that I'd choose. As such we'd normally end up in an awful resort in Spain where it was cheap and tacky, albeit still quite fun. Yes, it would be a beach holiday and yes, I'd feel pretty ashamed to be the fat one in the group. However it still wasn't enough to inspire me to make a change. That was until I was finally able to convince this group to go with me to Las Vegas, a party destination I'd had on my radar for years. I set out a plan whereby if they all agreed to save up for three years then it was affordable for the entire group. The long story cut short to this anecdote is that although they agreed and some started saving, all eventually dropped out and I ended up going to Vegas two years later with a friend who could afford it.

So then, Vegas was the catalyst that finally turned it all around for me. Towards the end of 2013 our flights were booked for May 2014. I knew then that if I started training in January, I'd have a decent shot at losing some weight in time for the holiday. By this stage in my life I had accepted the fact that I'd never again have the type of body I sported in my twenties (wrong!), but I at least hoped that I could have a flatter stomach so I wouldn't have to walk everywhere sucking in my gut. But seriously, how was this any different to the other boys' holidays I'd been on before? Well…

1. I'd dreamed of a guy's holiday in Vegas for years – anyone reading this who has been fortunate enough to go will understand. If you haven't been then get those flights booked NOW! You can thank me later…

2. When it finally came time to fly, it had already been years in the planning.

3. It was going to cost me thousands of pounds to go – buying clothes for the trip, the flights and hotel, a lot of spending money, etc. This was not your average trip to Tenerife!

4. Most importantly, when in Vegas I wanted to feel good about myself, actually scratch that, I wanted to feel amazing about myself. I didn't want to be 'the fat one' again.

5. I planned my trip with my good friend Scott who despite being seven years older than me, is one of those frustrating people in life who never falters from maintaining their diet and going to the gym. As a result Scott was already in fantastic condition. Next to him I would have simply been an embarrassment.

So, my motivation was firmly set there. I was obsessed with Vegas and in the months leading up to the trip it occupied my every thought. I committed myself to adhere to a four month plan of dieting and going to the gym in the morning before I started work. Although I'd previously preferred to train later in the day, I knew the only way to guarantee making it to the gym at this stage in life would be to do it before the rest of life's little distractions started. That is at least true of my example; you'll know best what would work for you.

Five days a week my alarm sounded two hours earlier than normal. Every morning I wanted to throw it out the window. However, each time I would open my eyes, start thinking of Las Vegas, and force myself out of bed so I could head for the gym. When at the gym I'd always work that little harder thinking of Vegas – it became a bit of a joke to call out such motivational phrases when trying to push out the final reps as "Girls in little bikinis!" There were also those occasions where I found myself on a treadmill suffering with yet another twenty minutes to go. Although I felt like stopping or at least slowing down the pace…that's right, I thought of Vegas and turned the speed up a bit more! Of course the gym was only part of the plan. Every time I walked past the snacks aisle in the supermarket and headed home with a car full of raw vegetables, I was thinking of Vegas.

This might sound like an unhealthy obsession to some. Actually the point is, I consciously allowed it to become all-consuming as I needed that drive to spur me on. Without it, when I felt hungry late at night, which historically has always been when I start to crave food, then I wouldn't have been able to stop myself from reaching for the cookie jar. Once you've achieved your goals, as I did, you'll be able to ease yourself back in to normal life again. By this stage your entire body will be reset, capable of processing food at an optimum level and will respond faster to exercise.

Some of you may be thinking that Las Vegas is not without its fair share of 'fatties.' Well clearly I'm not talking about hanging out in casinos with obese people driving around in their scooters, I'm talking about hitting the pool parties where it seems to be an unwritten rule that you only attend if you're suitably attractive.

In addition to the high motivation levels I'd installed in myself, I was very lucky to have Scott. Scott was due to go to Vegas with me. As such he was totally invested in my achieving my goal as he didn't want to go there with a fat guy. In a perverse way, he was almost as invested in my reboot as I was! Scott offered me the chance to start going to the gym with him. Suddenly the shoe was firmly on the other foot whereby the baton had passed to Scott to knock me back into shape, rather than in previous years where I found myself training others. The importance of having a training partner in this case was two-fold:

1. It's a great deal easier training with someone else when they're there to help keep you motivated and spur you on.

2. Even with Vegas firmly in my mind, there were still some mornings where I could have very easily stayed in bed. Knowing I had Scott waiting for me at the gym was yet more motivation to get up and force myself in to action.

So, part of my planning was choosing the right training partner…or perhaps this was more a case of luck! Actually Scott is a rather shrewd businessman with a number of men's' clothes shops so he had plenty of reason to keep me motivated. After a short space of time, literally none of my clothes fitted anymore, Scott then made a small fortune out of me as I needed a completely new wardrobe, much to his delight.

Now we've acknowledged the need to establish the right level of motivation, how are you going to achieve this? Take some time now or over the coming days to consider what goal you're going to set yourself. As I've stated before, don't simply answer that question with "I want to lose 10lbs" because that is not going to keep you away from the goodie cupboard on Monday night when you've got a craving! Consider and complete the following:

1. Set yourself a goal to work towards. If mine was to look good for a holiday in Vegas, consider what will get **you** out of bed in the morning. Is it to buy yourself an expensive item of clothing that is too small for you to wear at the moment? Do you already have a favourite outfit in your wardrobe that you haven't been able to squeeze in to for years but haven't had the heart to throw away? Perhaps you might want to book yourself a photo shoot so that you can look back on photos of yourself looking great when you're old and grey? Like Joe Cross and Jason Vale, are you suffering from ill health and want to improve this? Perhaps you'd like to follow my model and book your trip to Vegas? Whatever your cause, find it and commit yourself in full.

2. What can you do to help yourself achieve your goals? Do you find yourself a training partner like Scott? Do you hire a Personal Trainer? Do you have friends and family who can support you? What about the online support package such as

the example offered by Shaun T and his team? I might just clarify by saying that's a great option; however the teams behind online support can only go so far – they're not there to see you on a daily basis and are not going to come and pull the bacon sandwich out of your hands when you're crashing! Helping yourself might be as simple as removing all temptation from your home, i.e. throwing out all the snacks and takeout menus. For me I helped myself by putting a 'fat photo' on my fridge as a reminder of the consequences of opening it for the wrong things. I had Scott to keep me focused. I had Vegas firmly on my mind. I even had my Fat, Sick and Nearly Dead DVD ready to watch in case I needed a little extra inspiration. All these little things, silly as they might sound, all contributed to keeping me on track.

3. When I finally found the motivation to go back to the gym I knew I'd be entering a place full of people who were already in good shape. I admit this can be a little intimidating, particularly when you look like this:

When I went back to the gym I wore baggy clothes and covered as much of my body as possible. Part of mentally preparing yourself to start your transformation is to accept and embrace your starting point. If you're overweight or otherwise out of shape, then who cares? That's why you're wearing your gym clothes, you're wearing them to train and turn it all around. When I first started at the gym I knew some were sniggering at me, or openly mocking me when I'd have to have a long rest. I kept on telling myself that soon enough, I'd show them and sport a better body than they'd ever achieve. So don't worry about how others see you now, focus on how they'll see the new you in the near future.

4. Set yourself a plan on how you're going to achieve your transformation. If you're not planning on exercising and just want to focus on your diet (not that I'd recommend following this route), then you need only prepare for following the diet plan in this book. However remembering what I've stipulated

thus far, you may have decided to extract certain elements of the diet and incorporate it with your own plan. That is certainly your call to make. I can tell you what I've found that works, but you are the masters of your own destiny. If, however, you are going to include exercise as part of your regime (and good for you if this is the case), then decide what you want to do. Are you going to do it all in the gym? Will you be taking those long walks on a golf course? Are you taking up a sport? Game of squash, anyone? Would you see better results working out at home? A combination of all of these options and more? Do your research and decide what the best plan is for you. As I mentioned at the start, if you don't like doing something then the chances of you keeping it up are slim. I've been set programmes by trainers in the past which I haven't enjoyed; equally, just trying to go through the Insanity DVD's at home by myself didn't work. I'm most motivated when in a gym with others lifting weights. In this case that's exactly the option I chose and of course, is the one I've been able to stick with.

5. Now decide what you need in place before you start. In my case I needed to buy a juicer and a recipe book. As luck would have it my juicer came with a Jason Vale recipe book which was filled with around a hundred different options to choose from – and they're surprisingly delicious! Next I needed to sign up for a gym membership and plan the times I would train. I already owned the Insanity DVDs, which I planned on using on top of going to the gym. Finally, I also purchased some very basic home gym equipment with was part of the overall exercise plan I designed for myself. How about you? What are you going to need in order to get the ball rolling and commence your transformation?

Once you've effectively answered points 1 through 5 then you'll be ready to begin…and this is where it starts to get exciting!

Chapter 4: The Diet

We all know how I put on weight. There was no-one to blame but me. It was the result of this kind of abuse:

Actually one of my biggest downfalls was discovering home cookbooks and realising how much I enjoyed cooking. This led to a lot more eating…so beware!

Now that we've accepted the reality of my actions, let's proceed…

Let me be entirely clear: I am not a doctor and am only speaking to you based on commonly understood best practices. I would firmly suggest you all consult your local doctor prior to embarking on this potentially radical lifestyle change. I can't advise you from a medical standing on the nutritional values of the foods I'll advise you to eat. What I can do is tell you that since switching to this plan I feel so much better myself. The dry skin and joint pain I told you of earlier has all gone away. I've found my energy levels have gone through the roof and in general I actually feel great. For the short periods where I've left this diet in the past year, I've again started to feel lethargic and unmotivated. There was even an occasion where I had around four weeks without juicing regularly and my fingernails became flaky and rough – how odd, it's like my body was giving me a sign that it was missing the nutrients! They stayed that way for a couple of weeks. I knew I needed to go back to juicing, a few days later my fingernails were back to normal. Oh, and of course let us not lose sight of the fact that my diet and overall regime resulted in this:

Feeling as though you can trust me? Hopefully the answer is **YES!**

Before we get into my diet, here are a few pointers to consider:

- Eat for your body type. We are all different and have bodies that process food at different rates. If you have a high metabolism then you're going to want to eat larger amounts of food on a regular basis. If your metabolism is slower, and/or you're not able to exercise very much, well then you'll clearly want to eat a bit less than others. That being said, I wouldn't necessarily advise to eat less than is stipulated in my diet plan below, perhaps just consider your portion sizes. A good example is my friend Scott whom we've spoken about. Scott is very tall and naturally lean. In comparison to Scott I'm shorter and broader. Scott can therefore afford to eat more food than I can and stay lean, whereas I have to consider eating just as often, but foods that are not quite so high in calories – which if not burned off will transfer to my fat cells.

We've spoken often about Scott, so here he is:

Bear in mind Scott is forty three so he's not doing too badly!

- In the same token, first consider how active you are when you decide how much food to eat. Back to Scott, he's on his feet for most of the day racing around his clothes shops. With all that dashing about I would estimate he walks around three to five miles every day…before he's even left work! Most of us should be so lucky! Again by comparison, I'm mostly sat behind my laptop screen all day and thus expending far fewer calories. This then means I can't afford to eat as much as Scott, or if I do, then I need to spend more time in the gym. If not, I'll put on weight that won't be burned off as I'm not exercising as much. Exercise doesn't happen just in the gym, we're burning calories all day long.

- Every couple of months or so I like to take a week off. That means a full week of no dieting and no training. From my experience I've found my body needs time to recover, repair and will generally thank me for the break. You'll return to your exercise plan stronger, fitter and looking better than ever. It's the honest truth that after my 'break week' of stuffing myself full of burgers, chocolate, and everything else I fancy eating, I actually look better than when I'm dieting.

I'm afraid I can't explain why this happens and the irony just kills me. Yet somehow, it works!

- Eat according to the goals you want to achieve. If you're aiming to 'bulk up' and build vast amounts of muscle then you're going to need to eat considerably more to fuel your muscle growth, including consuming higher amounts of protein. My diet plan is more focused on losing weight and being athletic. Consider this in advance and plan accordingly. You may find it useful to start with my plan and then experiment as the months pass to find what works best for you. The amount of food you consume will also affect your energy levels. I'm informed that at the peak of his training regiment, the Olympic swimmer Michael Phelps turned to eating primarily Domino's pizza as it was the only food he could find that contained enough calories to support his training regime. That's pretty incredible! And before you get any funny ideas, unless you're planning on training for around ten hours per day, I would forget about the Domino's for a while. In line with eating according to your goals, remember that my diet is based on the concept of being health-based and allowing you to build and maintain a healthy appearance. If you're training to go on stage at a bodybuilding competition then this really isn't the one for you. It's all relative.

- There is a lot of advice out there on what supplements you should be taking. As a rule of thumb I don't take any unless I know I'm struggling to get them in my normal daily routine. Then this constitutes a daily fish oil tablet (I'm not a huge fan of oily fish so tend not to eat it) and a daily vitamin D pill during the winter. As I understand it, the only source of vitamin D is from the sun. I don't like taking other vitamin pills, because why should you need to if you're getting it all naturally from your diet? Actually there are many studies that have shown that overdosing on your vitamin count can be harmful. There's so much contradicting guidance out there so I prefer to keep it simple and just cover it through natural sources – I'd rather vitamins and nutrients in their natural form than from a man-made pill. Logical?

- I've spoken with a lot of Personal Trainers over the years, some of which are simply terrified of carbohydrates. "Don't eat carbs, they'll make you fat!" Well, we actually take our energy from carbs so I'm really not sure I agree with that at all. Again, let's focus on keeping it simple and eating in moderation. So long as you're not eating every meal with potatoes, rice, pasta, bread, and all the other so called 'taboo food groups,' I don't see this being an issue.

- There seems to be a big debate on whether you should drink milk, i.e. standard milk that comes from a cow. I was previously lucky to have a doctor in my family (on my ex-wife's side). Her grandfather is a world famous kidney specialist, if I'm not wrong then I believe he was still considered one of the world's leading specialists in his field even after he retired. He is a great advocate of drinking milk for its health benefits. I'd certainly be inclined to trust his judgment. In his mid-seventies he was still playing tennis most days, cycling to and from work, and I once found him climbing a tree in his garden to pick fruit! Myself, I like the taste so that is good enough for me. However if you speak to Personal Trainers then many will warn you off milk and suggest alternatives such as almond milk. To that, I'll again say, if you're aiming to hit 3% body fat and get on stage then maybe you should do some more research. If this is not the case then to those individuals I'd suggest "get a life!" Everything in moderation please, and pass me a pint of the semi-skimmed. I've continued to drink normal milk and it's done me no harm.

- Your body is comprised of roughly 60% water; you need to stay hydrated in order for it to run properly. Drinking plenty of water helps to flush toxins from your body. I've even been told it helps to combat the effects of ageing – which makes sense if you consider your skin needs to stay hydrated. The amount of water you need to drink depends on numerous factors, including your gender, size, how much you exercise, and so on. As a general rule of thumb, they say men in a day should drink 3 litres, women 2.2 litres. If you're juicing, this should be very easy to achieve.

- During the week, I do try to avoid drinking alcohol and fizzy (carbonated/soda) drinks. I mostly stick with juice (obviously the ones I prepare myself), water and milk. I do drink tea, however you'll want to try to limit the number of teas and coffees you drink per day, especially if you have them with milk (or cream!) and sugar. Let's say you drink six coffees in a day, each with two sugars. Well then that's a lot of added sugar to your day, particularly when you've been so good with the rest of your diet. If you can, do drink green tea which has been proven to be extremely healthy (I can't, it makes me retch!). Equally, with those fizzy you'll be amazed just how much sugar you're consuming in your seemingly harmless drink. I've prepared the following picture to give you an idea of just how much sugar there is in each serving:

Quite an eye opener, right? All that sugar equates to weight gain so try to limit your intake.

However, and this is a big one, **diet sodas are even worse and will make you fatter**. Shocking? Well, studies have revealed that artificially sweetened drinks place us at a higher risk of heart conditions and diabetes. And as stated, they will ultimately make you fatter. Here's how it happens:

o Artificial sweeteners are hundreds to thousands of times sweeter than regular sugar, activating our genetically programmed preference for sweet tastes more than any other substance.
o They trick your metabolism into thinking sugar is on its way. This causes your body to pump out insulin, the fat storage hormone, which lays down more belly fat.
o It also confuses and slows your metabolism down, so you burn fewer calories every day.
o It makes you hungrier and crave even more sugar and starchy carbs like bread and pasta.
o In animal studies, the rats that consumed artificial sweeteners ate more, their metabolism slowed, and they put on fourteen percent more body fat in just two weeks – even when eating fewer calories.
o In population studies there was a two-hundred percent increased risk of obesity in diet soda drinkers.

There you go, if it says 'diet' on the bottle, then avoid it like the plague!

- Try to avoid 'yo yo diets.' This means your weight regularly fluctuates up and down. I invite you to do further research on this topic, however essentially it is extremely detrimental to your health (placing you at increased risk of diabetes and heart conditions), and over time will lead to prolonged weight gain. Now that you're armed with your copy of From Fat to Fantastic, plan to make this your last diet scheme and stick to it.

- You may not have considered it before but where you live in the world might put you at more of a disadvantage or give you a head start on others. Consider the real-life example of my friend Luke. Luke and I were in the army together; he was always quite skinny but suffered with a pot-belly. Provided he ate relatively well and did minimal exercise then 'the pot' would always be kept well in check. Later in life Luke emigrated to Taiwan where he stayed for six years. There, he lived more in line with his Asian neighbours eating mostly vegetables, rice, noodles and proteins. He was also more active, it being quite normal to travel on a bicycle. Here's Luke in Taiwan:

Luke has since returned home to the UK where he has settled nicely back in to our classic way of life. He has swapped his bike for a car so doesn't get much (if any) exercise. Also he's returned to eating his favourite English foods, mostly heavy, stodgy pastry-based foods such as pies, Cornish pasties, bread, pasta and all the other usual suspects. Oh, and don't forget the tea & biscuits! In less than a year, Luke has transformed from his picture of health seen before, to this:

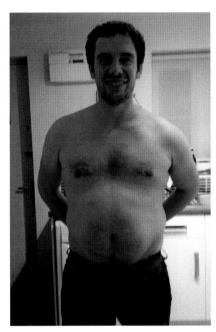 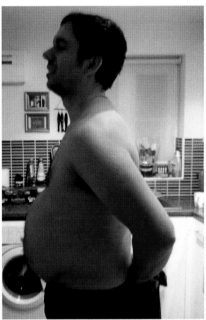

The scary thing about the side profile picture is Luke is standing naturally; he's not even pushing his belly out for effect. If I ever get a chance to write From Fat to Fantastic 2, then prepare to see Luke's results as I'll be taking him under my wing and helping him to lose this weight. This will be an interesting experiment as Luke has never been a fan of the gym, thus I'll have to plan his training regime based on his preferences rather than mine. We'll document it every step of the way so look forward to seeing how he does.

Now to my absolute best piece of advice, arguably the key to making all this work…

At various points I've alluded to the 80-20 rule, and being able to eat everything you want - or more accurately - not having to cut your favourite foods from your diet. I believe it's essential that you don't cut these foods out, or, as I've done so many times in the past, you'll throw a huge tantrum, push aside your juicer and head straight for the ice cream. Once you've hit this stage it can take a while (and much weight gain) to come back, whereupon you'll have to start all over again. So, allow yourself a cheat day or two.

Some people I know allow themselves one cheat meal per week, others are even more strict and will allow themselves only a single cheat on their plate – so they might have some fries with their chicken breast once a week. Again, it's all relative and depends on what you're working towards.

For me, I can't manage living this way, you may be stronger willed than I. If that's the case, then well done and good luck to you. Essentially, I can manage from Monday morning through to Friday night. As soon as Friday night arrives, that's it, bring on the pizza and chocolate brownies! Offer me lean white meat for my dinner and there'll be very serious trouble! I'll eat what I like from Friday night until Monday morning and then I feel totally satisfied and ready to start being good all over again. If anything, by Monday morning I'm starting to feel a bit guilty and can't wait to eat healthily and get back to the gym. Alternatively I could restrict myself to a single cheat meal or nothing at all and be left craving all the time. If you feel that way then you know you're in 'the danger zone.'

When I attended the screening of Fat, Sick and Nearly Dead 2, Joe Cross was answering questions from the audience. He got on to the topic of Hybrid Diets (which is similar to the one I follow) and spoke about the times to let yourself go and indulge in these types of processed foods. A woman in the audience questioned Joe on this and was quite aggressive in demanding Joe answer how he can endorse eating any processed food at all. Joe handled the question calmly and very well. I, on the other hand, wanted to shake her by the shoulders and remind her that likely ninety-five percent of people could never manage to avoid these foods indefinitely. Like me, the majority will soon falter. When I was in training for Vegas I remember lying in bed and fantasizing about spaghetti bolognaise and BBQ ribs…yes, it's a bit sad really! If you can manage without processed foods then good for you, if you're anything like me then I strongly recommend adopting the 80-20 rule in whatever form works best for you.

Note, for anyone not familiar with the term 'processed food', it basically refers to the transformation of raw ingredients, by physical or chemical means, into food. So the obvious candidates are crisps, chocolates, cheese, bread, pasta, and so on. For unprocessed foods, think of your vegetables being pulled directly from the ground, or meat being taken straight off the bone. You've got the general gist? Of course that's not to say that all processed foods are bad for us. I eat natural yoghurt which (so we're told) is extremely good for us. It's just common sense. Avoid the can of spam and instead opt for a lean piece of steak.

On that note, let's look at my diet in more depth…

My diet plan is broken down in to three key phases. In order to follow this you will need a juicer and a blender. The better the juicer you buy, the more juice you'll get out of your fruits and vegetables. I've just bought myself a new juicer made by Sage which seems to be working very well. If money is tight and you can't afford to buy a juicer then it's not the end of the world. Another friend of mine only uses a blender for his vegetables and fruits and he's in great shape. However do try to go with the juicer option if you can. The Nutribullet seems now to be very much in vogue given you keep more of the fibre you'd lose through juicing. Whilst I'm content with my juicer, I can't argue the logic to this one. You'll decide what direction you want to take for yourself.

Phase 1 (Weeks 1 and 2)

Phase 1 is designed to get your weight down fast (if that's applicable to your case) and achieve initial results that will then motivate you to keep on going. It's also intended to reset your taste buds, which is applicable to all. As unbelievable as that might sound, it's absolutely true. By my second weekend during Phase 1 I was gorging myself on a Sunday evening (clearing out all the cookies so I wouldn't have any temptation during the week) and I reached a point where I simply couldn't eat any more. My body had literally reached the stage where it said "Hey Gav, that's enough sugar now, how about some fresh vegetables?" Even though it was the weekend – my time to eat what I want – I was actually craving a juice as my system had been reset. Amazing!

For the first two weeks you'll need to replace your breakfast and lunch for juice. For each meal replacement I was having about one litre of juice. I'd sip it constantly through the day and this would help me avoid feeling hungry.

Now, be under no illusions, the first few days are **hard**. I felt disorientated, weak and very hungry. However, stay strong and push through it, this doesn't last for long and you get to eat in the evening.

For my evening meal I would I would have a healthy, balanced dinner whilst avoiding all processed foods. My favourite at this time was to make a stir fry full of big chunky vegetables, a little sauce of some kind for flavour and a small portion of protein such as white meats (fish, chicken, turkey, etc.), or a red meat (beef, lamb, etc.). To give the statement of 'a small portion' some context, if I'd normally eat two chicken breasts for my dinner, then I cut it down to one chicken breast, or even half a chicken breast on occasion. I'd then focus more on filling up with the vegetables. Some of my other regular meals included venison meatballs with salad and new potatoes, or chicken with vegetables and brown rice.

If I found myself struggling then I'd allow myself a snack of one of the following:

- Either a single rice cake or apple with a teaspoon of natural peanut butter.

- A small handful of either cashews or almonds. For these I actually went with the salted/roasted versions. Hey, I was being so good in every other area that I needed a bit of flavour and didn't feel this would amount to excess salt considering I was barely getting any elsewhere. Moderation!

- A single piece of fruit.

Now, try not to snack too much, one or two snacks per day should be your limit.

When I started Phase 1 I weighed 16.5 stone (105kg/231lbs), had a 38 inch waist and looked like this (taken the night before I began):

By the end of Phase 1 (so in the space of two weeks), I'd lost a staggering 1.5 stone (10kg/22lb) and had dropped to a 36 inch waist. I couldn't believe the weight had fallen off so quickly, particularly as I'd eaten so much at the weekends. I'd lost an incredible amount of weight without having to go without the foods I love so much…perfect! Sadly I didn't take a photo at the end of Phase 1; make sure you do so that you can track your progress.

Probably the starkest indication that I was changing occurred at the end of Week 1 (again on Sunday night). I knew I was heading back in to my healthy regime in the morning so went to bed on a fully belly of pizza…only to have one of the worst night's sleep I can remember in recent years – I woke up three times desperate for water having consumed all the excess salt, was generally uncomfortable and woke up in the morning feeling like my old, heavy and lethargic self. I couldn't wait for a juice in the morning to cleanse my system.

As to the weight loss stated above, it is absolutely accurate and true. I was carrying a lot of weight my body didn't need and had immediately started training very hard. This allowed me to lose the weight this fast.

Phase 2 (Weeks 3 to 6)

By this stage you should have lost a decent amount of weight and be able to see the results taking effect. This is of course assuming you're following the guidance as I've set it out for you. My mother decided she wanted to lose weight following my diet model so I wrote out a plan for her. After a few weeks she was complaining it wasn't working so I asked her what she was eating. She proceeded to tell me that she was having her juices…and a few slices of toast for breakfast (with lashings of butter, knowing my mother), Ryvita for lunch (so processed bread), and the list went on with a few other snacks here and there. Oh, and I think my father also got blamed for eating nuts and chocolate in front of her in the evening which made her crack and eat the same! Seriously, if you're going to see any results then you must be disciplined and follow Phases 1 and 2 to the letter. This will reboot your entire system and change the way your body processes food. In the past if I ate a big meal I would bloat and seem to convert it all straight to fat. Now that all the hard work has been done, I can afford to fall off the wagon for weeks at a time before my body starts to show any signs of abuse.

So again, by this stage you should have lost a decent amount of weight…

Now you can start to reintroduce more food back in to your system. Start your day with a smoothie. Feel free to create your own concoctions, my three regulars options were –

Option 1:   1 x banana or a handful of berries
             Skimmed (fat free) milk
             Protein powder (intended to support my training regime)
             4 x tbsp natural yoghurt

Option 2:   skimmed milk
             Protein powder
             Ground oats (available from any good fitness shop or website)

Option 3:   3 x egg white omelettes with two vegetables (I mostly favoured either tomatoes and onions, or peppers and onions)

I'd then repeat the same as seen in Phase 1, i.e. a juice for lunch, a well-balanced dinner, and a choice of the three snacks.

During Phase 2 everything started to feel that much easier and having a smoothie or juice for breakfast felt as natural to me as having a bowl of cereal. For days when I was on the road traveling and couldn't juice, I would simply have a healthy salad instead. The point was I found myself unconsciously reaching for salads rather than staring at pizza through shop windows with a glint in my eye. One of my favourites came from Pret A Manger (a popular coffee shop akin to Starbucks), who serve a superfood salad. Interestingly I had previously tried it and found it tasted awful. However after I'd reset my taste buds, I found it delicious – how weird! Most days I would be able to juice, I'd simply prepare it beforehand and take it with me, however there were some occasions where I'd be away from home for several days at a time so would therefore run out of juice.

I found myself also getting lighter which in turn allowed me to train harder in the gym, again increasing the overall results of my transformation.

As before, from Friday night I'd allow myself the opportunity to have whatever I wanted right through to Monday morning. I hope my Personal Trainer Jason never reads this book or he'll go mad that I eat this many cheats! However, perhaps he'll also consider the reality more of the 80-20 rule.

By the end of Week Six I'd lost a further 0.7 stone (5kg/11lb), taking my total weight loss to 2 stone (15kg/33lbs), well just over 2 stone to be accurate. Don't forget of course that by this stage I'd been back in the gym for six weeks building muscle, muscle as we know weighs more than fat. Had I not been building muscle then my weight loss would have been greater, although the results wouldn't necessarily have been better. In addition, my waist had dropped further to 34 inches – that's four inches off my belly in six weeks!

Phase 3

Phase 3 is essentially an indefinite period of time, or if you choose to stick with the programme, the rest of your life – for want of a better phrase. By this stage you should have reset your system and can return back to a normal way of life by eating real foods. However, don't give up on the juice entirely; don't forget the health benefits it offers. I as a rule still try to juice three to four times per week. Mostly I'll add it in as a healthy part of my diet rather than using it as a meal replacement. I most often have a litre of juice at some point in the day to replace a snack.

Just because you're now eating properly again doesn't mean you can stop eating healthily. Consider what you've learned thus far and apply it to your new healthy lifestyle. An average day in my life during Phase 3 might look something like this:

Breakfast: A protein shake after the gym and then either a smoothie, a juice, or eggs.

Lunch: Some form of salad. One of my favourites consists of chicken, couscous (giant brown couscous is my favourite), feta cheese, carrot, cucumber, toasted pine nuts, pomegranate seeds and lemon juice.

The point with salads is they don't have to be boring – break away from the illusion of lettuce and a few other vegetables. Yes I still enjoy these and do eat them, but it would be pretty dull to have to eat that every day.

Snack: A small handful of cashews or almonds, or natural peanut butter on a rice cake or apple.

Dinner: A healthy meal and balanced unprocessed meal.

Snack: A piece of fruit.

I continued to train and stick to my diet, by Week 10 I looked like this:

I'm sure you'll agree the results are rather stark for such a short space of time.

Remember, as part of my plan to 'Get Motivated,' I was working towards a four month plan of getting in shape for my trip to Las Vegas. As I mentioned, I had initially hoped to flatten my stomach and lose a few extra pounds. Even after Phase 1 I knew I was going to smash that initial goal so just continued to work harder and harder. By the time I was due to fly to Vegas I took my final transformation photos and looked like this:

You can see just how far my transformation went. In four months that really wasn't a bad effort at all.

Now for a few 'top tips' to finish this Chapter –

- Again in line with my complete disclosure, in the four month build up to Vegas I wasn't always perfect with the 80-20 rule, some days I did slip. This might be in the form of a chocolate bar during the week, or I might lose it completely and order a large pizza and side dishes. Jason (my trainer) would always know when it happened as I'd come in to the gym in the morning with 'a carb hangover,' i.e. I'd be lethargic and tired.

He scorns me for allowing myself cheat meals (including at the weekend) and points out how good I could look if I didn't have so many. Now the reality is Jason is absolutely right. However, as I've maintained, we're all different and have to set our targets based on our own capabilities. I can't resist food! For yourselves, if you find yourself breaking in the week then it's not the end of the world so don't have a tantrum and quit altogether. Do try to avoid these extra cheats if you can, but accept that provided it's not all the time, it's not going to ruin the rest of the hard work you've put in. However, do not allow yourself to fail during Phase 1 and ideally, not during phase 2. You need this initial period to reset your system.

- For your juices, focus more on 'green juices' with higher amounts of green super foods such as spinach, broccoli and kale. The fruit juices taste great but are still full of natural sugars. By the time you've added some fruit to your green juices then they tend to sweeten up very nicely and taste great. Again I'm not going to attempt to recreate the wheel and offer you a variety of juice recipes as there are already plenty of others out there. I recommend you look for a recipe book from either Joe Cross or Jason Vale. I've tried both and they're very good. For me, I've actually got to the stage where I've stopped preparing my juices based on flavour, preferring to focus on targeting the amount of different vegetables that go in, thus the nutrients I take out. You don't have to do this, if anything I do recommend you start with recipe books and trial which ones taste best to you. My standard recipe is as follows:

Ingredients: 2 x large bags of spinach
                   1 x large bag of kale
                   3 x courgettes
                   1 x medium bag of carrots
                   1 x pack of celery
                   3 x peppers (red, yellow and green)
                   1 x parsnip
                   1 x lettuce
                   3 x broccoli stems

1 x raw beetroot
A chunk of fresh root ginger
9 x apples
1 x pineapple (remove the rind)
6 x pears
4 x limes (peeled. Try to keep as much of the white pith under the skin as possible – somehow I discovered that a bread knife works best for this)
3 x lemons

Note I make my juices in bulk, you'll get several litres out of this recipe.

- Your juice can go with you anywhere, there are no excuses. As this photo demonstrates, I'm sat on the train in First Class turning down the offer of free bacon sandwiches and instead opting to continue with my healthy diet

- If you have a lot of weight to lose, as I did, remember your body is going to keep on evolving for several months. As my waist had dropped from a 38" to a 34" between January and May, I was forced to replace all my jeans and trousers. By October I found again that none of my jeans fit me properly – they were hanging off my bum and were baggy in the leg. I went back in to see Scott for a new pair and found that I'd dropped a further two inches off my waist and now needed to buy 32" waist jeans. I found this amazing as since my return from Las Vegas I'd neither trained as hard, nor had I been quite so diligent with my diet. However what I had done, as I mentioned before, was reset my body so now I was able to process my food intake in a far more efficient way. Over time my body had continued to do the work for me and I've lost even more weight. Seriously people, believe in the system as it really does work!

- Phases 1 and 2 constitute a low amount of food. The good news is I can tell you now that I was not eating enough food, especially considering how hard I was working in the gym. However, the purpose of this book is to demonstrate exactly what I did as part of my transformation. Ultimately it's only six weeks of your life, and then you can get back to eating enough to properly sustain your body and personal routine.

- Although we've centred our discussions on food consumption, it should go without saying that you need to apply the same rules to what you drink during the week. If you're sat drinking pint after pint of beer every night then it's highly unlikely that you're going to see any great results in your waistline! If you must drink during the week then I might suggest a glass or two of wine. Probably the best option is Vodka and soda or slim line tonic, this drink carries very few calories. Moderation please.

- Whatever you do, don't put onion in your juice. I experimented once with that…once was too much! Suffice to say it tasted awful! Also, beware of putting fruits through with their skins on. Some are fine, but as a general rule I take the skins off fruit that I wouldn't normally eat. When I first started juicing I left the skins on, this was another serious faux pas when juicing limes – to say it tasted bitter is a real understatement. Whoops!

- As you may have gathered by now, I have a very busy schedule and need to travel regularly for my job. This then doesn't lend itself well to being at home to juice. Equally the prospect of having to juice every day wasn't very appealing. In my mind it meant too many trips to the supermarket (otherwise the vegetables/fruits might start to go off) and just too much effort having to prepare them daily (given the mess and cleaning times). To get around this I'd make all my juices at the weekend in one big batch. I'd then portion the juice out in to freezer bags and put them in the freezer. If I was at home it was as simple as taking one out the night before so it was ready for the morning. Alternatively if I was travelling then I could pack them in a large Tupperware and take them in my suitcase wherever I went. Note, it's easier to add them to your Tupperware in advance otherwise it's hard to fit them in (once in a bag they'll freeze in odd shapes). Also separate the freezer bags in a second plastic bag or they may stick together and tear when they start to defrost.

I have been asked the question before - whether you can freeze your juices whilst retaining the nutritional value. The answer is yes, you can and no, you don't lose anything. However, once out of the freezer you do have to consume the juice within the space of twenty-four hours. Also, you need to keep the juice in a dark place and out of direct sunlight. Even better than freezer bags are aluminium water bottles as they will do a much better job of protecting your juice from the damaging effects of light. If you break these rules then you're effectively just drinking flavoured water and have lost all the nutrient rich qualities.

- Try recreating some of your favourite meals in a new and healthier way. I've done this with a number of dishes by swapping some of the ingredients for healthier options. It might not taste quite the same as before, but will still serve to make your weekday meals a bit more interesting – you'll soon tire of stir-fry! One good example is to roast a chicken and rather than serve it with potatoes and gravy, try serving it with an interesting salad (not just lettuce and tomatoes) Here's a great example of how I make a healthy chilli:

Ingredients: 400g Chicken mince (instead of beef)
                 400g Turkey mince (instead of pork)
                 2 x Large white onions (roughly chopped)
                 1 x Tin of kidney beans
                 2 x Tins of plum tomatoes
                 2 x Tins of chopped tomatoes
                 1 x Tin of baked beans (optional)

6 x Cloves of garlic
A selection of vegetables
Tomato puree, tomato ketchup, Worcester sauce, chili paste, herbs (I prefer to make mine with a ready pack you find in a supermarket for chili), salt and pepper

You can basically make your chilli according to your own recipe, however this is how I like to make mine. The key here is you've swapped the meat (which is already fairly healthy) for a super healthy poultry option. Also you're adding a lot more vegetables.

- Start by browning your meat in batches in a large frying pan and draining off any excess liquid. Transfer the meat in to a large saucepan.
- Fry the onions until they start to soften. Add the crushed garlic cloves for the last minute and then add both to your saucepan with the meat.
- Add the tomatoes and beans to the saucepan.
- Now season generously with the tomato puree, tomato ketchup, Worcester sauce, chili paste, herbs, salt and pepper (all according to taste).
- Your selection of vegetables can be anything you like. I normally go for whatever I have left in the fridge – perhaps some broccoli, peppers, spinach, etc. You may choose to cook them whole in your chilli, I however prefer my chilli to have the constituency of a classic chilli. So, I put all these vegetables in to a blender with a little water and proceed to liquidize them. I then add the liquid to the pot with everything else.
- Bring the contents of your saucepan to the boil and then simmer for around two hours. If you've liquidized the vegetables then it will be quite wet to begin with so you'll need to reduce it down to the right consistency.
- Leave the chilli to mature for at least twenty-four hours and serve on brown rice. Or, if you're being particularly good then you can choose to serve it with vegetables.
- Enjoy!

Do you remember Louise who I spoke of in an earlier chapter – the nutritionist I dated for a while? Louise introduced me to a lot of new healthy meals which quite frankly, tasted just as good as any of the foods I treated myself to at the weekend. Some of these options included:

- Roasted vegetables served with halloumi cheese and tomato chutney. This is a great lunch option.
- Pan fried pork steaks marinated in a herb and spice rub, served on a bed of bok choy. I didn't even realise I liked bok choy as much as I do until she introduced me to this dish! Unfortunately she wouldn't share her recipe (it's patented to her company) so this might take some experimentation. Stand by for a whole new set of recipes in From Fat to Fantastic 2!
- Possibly my favourite was her healthy lasagne. This was basically lean mince, thinly sliced vegetables (to replace the pasta) and seasoning (to replace the white sauce). Add some cheese on top and it's done. I couldn't believe how good this tasted, it was almost better than classic lasagne. There are plenty of recipes available for this on Google so why not give it a try.

Louise runs her own small business writing diet plans for her clients. You might choose to consult a local nutritionist for new ideas on healthy and delicious meal options. For myself I simply bought a number of cookbooks designed as being health conscious. Try Googling 'nutritious grains' as a suitable starting point and you'll soon get the idea.

And so that's it, there's your new diet. Feel free to experiment a little over the months and find what works best for you.

Chapter 5: Time to Start Exercising

So, you've decided to include some physical training as part of your new healthy lifestyle. **Good choice!** The simple fact is that without exercising, you're never going to maximize your potential. If you're going through the hardship of rebooting your diet and lifestyle habits, well then you may as well go the 'whole hog' and treat yourself to a few push-ups before bedtime...

As I've stated on numerous occasions throughout the course of this book, it's essential that you choose a training regime that works for you, i.e. something you'll enjoy and will keep on doing. I personally find swimming lengths in a pool very boring. Swimming is great exercise that doesn't put any impact on our joints, unlike jogging as a prime example where your ankles and knees bear the brunt of a constant pounding. However put me in a pool and tell me to swim fifty lengths and I'll typically spend the first ten telling myself to just get on and finish it...the next ten considering excuses for why I should stop and go home...and the next thirty invariably won't happen as I'll be in the car headed for my sofa. By contrast, put me on a squash court for an hour and by the end I'll be begging for just a couple more games, or feeling so stimulated by the fun I've had during the game that I suggest we finish our workout off by running home! Similarly, My ex-wife hated training with weights yet periodically convinced herself she could change her ways...all we ended up with was my paying a monthly gym membership for her that was never used and a cupboard full of expensive kettle bells covered in dust. What she did enjoy was yoga and Pilates, we switched to that and she was able to keep up her routine with no problem at all.

Consider all the lessons you've learned thus far from the previous chapters. As part of your planning stage, now consider what the best way to exercise for **you** is.

So, you'll need to decide what type of body you want to build and then be realistic in your expectations. It's no good going line dancing twice a week and then wondering why you've not developed bulging biceps. As I said earlier, I grew up on Arnold Schwarzenegger films and was fascinated by 1980's muscular action movie stars. As such, when I grew up I started lifting weights to emulate their physiques. So what kind of look do you aspire to? Would you like a body like a boxer? If this is the case then the best answer will surely be to join a boxing gym and start performing the same routine. You don't necessarily need to get in the ring, but you can still spend hours punching bags, sprinting up mountains and chasing chickens (you may need to watch the Rocky films to make sense of those references!). Perhaps you think the broad shoulders and toned bodies of swimmers are best? Well then, get in your trunks and dive in the pool! If you're going to follow this piece of advice then I suggest you to do a little research first on the different routines each athlete adheres to. For swimmers, it's not quite as simple as swimming hundreds of lengths. Like most others, they'll also spend a decent amount of time in the gym lifting weights. If you've ever seen Tiger Woods on TV (I'll be shocked if the answer is no!), you'll see he's quite a big guy. This is the result of his spending hours in the gym lifting weights to increase his power and to improve his game on the golf course.

As a general rule of thumb doctors typically recommend we get a minimum of thirty minutes exercise per day, five times per week. In addition to the weight loss benefits, it also promotes a healthy heart, reduces the risk of disease and improves our overall well-being. Now they don't appear to specify what exercise you should do beyond anything that gets your heart rate up. On that basis all exercise that leaves you out of breath and sweaty is good exercise. And yes, that includes sex! Of course, like with anything else it does depend on how you do it. It's not much use going to the gym and sitting on an exercise bike reading a magazine whilst peddling gently for half an hour - I can't begin to tell you how much those people annoy me!

Likewise if your contribution to sex consists of you lying on your back for an hour screaming "Harder" and "Faster" then...

1. You're probably a pretty bad lover.

and

2. You've unlikely earned yourself a pass to miss the gym that day.

So, you're probably wondering what actually is the best form of exercise to build the perfect body? Well, again it depends on what you want to achieve. However in terms of all-round benefits, weight training is the answer. I simply can't think of a better way to develop your muscles and build a well-rounded, sculpted physique. However it's not quite as simple as picking up a set of dumbbells and going at it, there's definitely more of a science involved.

If you've ever been to a gym and seen those guys having a chat with their friends, checking themselves out in the mirror for ages, or sat for long periods of time resting between their sets, then wipe this image from your mind as **this is not part of your future**.

At a very basic level the rule with body building is if you want to get big, then you lift heavy weights with a lower number of reps (six to eight reps), if you're aiming or definition then you lift lighter weights for a higher number of reps (ten to eighteen). That's a very basic explanation. We'll not blow your mind at this stage by talking of super-setting, pyramiding and all the other fun techniques! All you need to worry about for now is the most effective routine for maximizing your results is to perform high intensity, explosive routines. So get used to this concept as **this is part of your future**.

Every six to eight weeks I change my routine. One routine might be designed towards building muscle (bulking), and then I'll move on to another for toning the muscle (stripping). However, whatever style of routine I do, I do it at a high intensity. This means I lift the heaviest weights I can but allow myself very little rest – around sixty seconds at a maximum, or the time it takes my training partner to complete his set. As soon as my partner puts down the weight, I step in and start my set. You can even make your routine harder by cutting the rest out altogether.

Just ensure you're working as hard as you can and cutting out all those long rests. That's the real key.

If you've made the effort to get out of your chair and put on your trainers/sneakers (the hardest part of any workout), then you might as well train as hard as possible and make it count. I have a Personal Trainer called Jason (we mentioned him in the last chapter). Jason is a fantastic guy, and is extremely knowledgeable and passionate about his industry. In the past year he has taught me new exercise routines and diets that I'd previously never seen. This re-emphasises my point that you truly never stop learning. Jason and I often laugh as he says "You love to be smashed (meaning I like to be worked to breaking point!)" And yes, he's absolutely right. If I'm not getting that then why am I paying him good money? I've not hired him for a gossip and a potter around the gym, I can do that myself. Schedule permitting, I'll train with Jason once or twice per week. Obviously I'm quite capable of training myself, and training hard. However, I choose to see Jason as I know he'll force me to work that much harder. Of course I'm still training most days with Scott, but I like to mix things up with Jason as his style is slightly different. Scott and Jason both push me to my limits, however they both have slightly different areas where they'll focus more, or are otherwise more lenient. They both have little favourites in their arsenals which I'd avoid if I was left to my own devices, such as finishing my weight routines with a sprint session on the treadmill, a 2000m best effort on the rowing machine, or the dreaded tyre flipping sessions. Mixing things up between these two 'beast masters' ensures I shock all areas of my body. Say hello to Jason:

Now, I'd say (and I'm sure most of you will agree), that Jason is in the best shape of all of us. Well, given this is both his profession and he spends most of his time in the gym I would certainly hope so! However, Jason also follows a very different diet to the one I've set out in this book. His shape is certainly more attuned to that of a bodybuilder that requires more preparation time for many smaller and regular meals. Given my work schedule, this is harder for me to follow. However, as part of my continued studies I intend to trial it. I'll be investigating both how following it affects my physique and the associated health properties. In preparation for From Fat to Fantastic 2, I'll undertake Jason's methods and will document the results (more on that later). Jason is convinced his methods will take me to the next level…and regularly chastises me for not realising my true potential (he's such a moaner!) In the meantime, don't feel as though you're missing out. As you've seen, my diet plan works and there should be no doubt in terms of its nutritional properties. At this stage we should all start by focusing on our health; achieving the ultimate 'beach body' will be a secondary consideration.

As an unrelated item, one other pleasant by-product of your new life might be you'll make some new friends. When I began this process I didn't know Scott very well. Now we're very close and I've made other very good friends through the gym; a small group of us now regularly hang out:

Back to the gym - with Jason's 'no nonsense' approach to training, which fortunately mirrors my own attitude. As I've said, if you're going to pay for a trainer then make sure you're getting your money's worth from them. I recently discussed this with another of my close friends, Dave, who is also a Personal Trainer. We agreed that the majority of Personal Trainers are too afraid to push their clients hard for fear that they'll be scared off and won't return. Dave is far stricter than this and pushes his clients until they collapse. We laughed as he regaled me with stories of having people laid on their backs with him holding their legs above their heads – allowing the blood to return to their head and for a speedier recovery, or more accurately so they don't pass out. I respect him all the more for his approach!

Now, I am a firm believer in pushing yourself as far as possible. I've already stressed the point that the harder you work, the greater your results will be. If I'm crawling out of the gym at the end of my session then I know I've done well! However, I do recommend knowing your own limits and not pushing yourself too far, particularly if you're new to exercise or have had a prolonged gap since training. When I first went back to the gym at the start of the year I obviously struggled. For the first two days I managed to make it halfway through my session with Scott, then I'd find myself feeling faint and actually had to go and lie down in the changing room (much to the amusement of others), or at least sit down for a while until I stopped feeling quite so sick and dizzy. Over the space of two weeks I was gradually able to increase the intensity of my training, moving from walking on the treadmill to a gentle jog, and as more time passed I was able to keep up with Scott and sprint. These things do take time, so be careful and don't expose yourself to the risk of injuries.

Okay, let's move on and start to discuss the right way to train. It is not my intention to document every conceivable training routine, or even cover all the exercise plans I've followed over the past year. Unfortunately to do so would effectively constitute an entire book in itself. What I will do for now is explain the best methods of training and offer you a few basic routines that will get you started. We'll 'bust a few myths' on what does and doesn't work and point you in the right direction for further advice. Again, if this book is successful then I plan to write a follow-up which delves much deeper in to training routines and healthy recipes for your diet.

Let's kick off the aforementioned promise by talking about my good friend James. James is a plumber so benefits from being quite active throughout the day, and he is already very diligent in his diet. Whilst James wasn't interested in exploring my diet plan, he did express a desire to improve his physique. We discussed what he wanted to achieve and concluded that he didn't want to build large muscles; rather he aimed to become more toned. We then discussed what he could do to get there. James works long hours so doesn't have the time to go to the gym. He also suffers with his knees meaning he can't run. I suggested James might substitute running for swimming, however we ultimately concluded the only training he was prepared to commit to was a routine he could do from home. Armed with this knowledge I proposed the following:

- I instructed James to purchase the following equipment for his house:

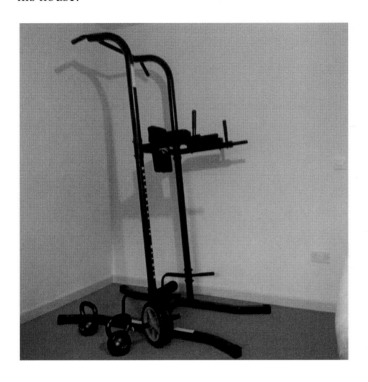

Even without the kettle bells and abs wheel seen on the floor, it's actually possible to get a complete upper body workout from this single piece of equipment. If need be then your legs can be trained without the use of gym equipment, or by using things around the house. Key exercises for the pull-up station pictured include pull-ups (or heaves); various core exercises, dips, push ups and sit ups.

Although James will admit he didn't follow the routine I set him to the letter (mostly due to time constraints), he did still manage to complete his own transformation. Here he is pictured at Week 1 and Week 10:

Believe it or not, he's actually flexing in both photos. What a great achievement, again in such a short space of time. And remember, he did nothing different with his diet; he simply started to follow (for the most part) a very simple exercise plan.

As well as being delighted with his results, I was happy to see a change in my friend's personality. James was suddenly a new man. He was happier, more confident and outgoing than ever. His physique began to improve, and as a by-product he started to take more pride in the rest of his appearance from the clothes he wore, to his grooming regime. Bizarrely, the better James felt about his body, the better his life became. His outward confidence led to his being more comfortable talking to women, this in itself had some rather positive results! But seriously, perhaps we can all relate to this? I know myself that when I was fat, I felt anything but sexy or confident. Even my sex life suffered as I wasn't happy being seen naked (and I certainly didn't have the 'energy' of my younger, slimmer self). Of course, having continued with the programme, James' physique continues to improve to this day. Having lived through James' scenario myself, I know just how this sense of well-being and new found pride can enrich our lives. It may be as simple as losing some weight and feeling better about ourselves; however increased confidence can lead us to the most unlikely places we never thought possible. Which version of yourself do you want to be? The timid version hiding away and hoping something good will come along? Or the ultra-confident Alpha who throws open the door and bellows "Everybody relax…I'm here!" Trust me, the latter version is a lot more fun!

For James, I set the following routine based on training four to five days per week (I think he managed on average three to four days per week). Don't worry if you don't understand the routine below, I'll explain later how to perform the exercises:

Morning routine:

- 20 x Push-ups
- 60 x Crunches > 15 x leg lifts
- 20 x Push-ups
- 50 x Station sit-ups
- 20 x Push-ups
- 20 x V-sits (weighted)
- 20 x Push-ups

As I advised James, these are the number of repetitions (reps) you should aim for. If you can't do this many then build up gradually. When you're used to the routine it should only take around fifteen minutes to complete. I don't know anyone who can't find fifteen minutes in their day for a quick burst of exercise!

Main routine:

- 20 x Kettle bell squats > 20 x scissor lunges
- 3 x Sets wide reverse grip pull-ups (10 x reps) > station vertical leg raises (15 x reps)
- 3 x Sets narrow reverse grip pull-ups (10 x reps) > station knee raises (15 x reps)
- 3 x Sets pull-ups (10 x reps) > lying leg raise with vertical lift (15 x reps)
- 20 x Kettle bell lunges > 20 x jumping squats
- 3 x Sets station dips (10 reps) > core pole twists (100 x twists)

- 20 x Station push-ups > Van Dammes (30 x reps)
- 20 x Station push-ups > single leg bench lunge kettle bell touchdown (10 x each leg)
- 20 x Station push ups > wood cutters (10 reps each side)
- 10 x Core wheel extensions

As before, if you can't do the number of reps I've specified then don't worry, just do the maximum you're capable of and over time, you'll get stronger. I might do this routine myself as part of a second workout for the day (having already been to the gym in the morning). As I'll complete a lot of cardio and high intensity training in the gym, I like to do this routine over the space of around ninety minutes while I watch a film. However, if this is the only routine you're doing in a day then you should keep your rest time short and power through it – you'll certainly get your heart rate up by the time this one is done! I suggest you should be able to easily complete it within the space of forty minutes. Add that to your morning routine and you've spent around an hour training...again, that's really not that bad now is it? Five days a week equals a total of five hours – there's twenty-four hours in a single day! It's nothing in the grand scheme of things and look what it did for James in a matter of weeks. Come on people, no more excuses!

Before I explain all the exercises in detail, let me offer you a few pointers:

- With some of the exercises I've instructed to use a weight (kettle bells). You can make all of these exercises harder by adding weights or easier by not using the weight. Find the level that is right for you.

- For this routine I find kettle bells to be the most practical. However you can use other weights, such as dumbbells, or anything else you might have at home that you can safely use. When I'm exercising in hotel rooms I tend to pick up chairs or whatever I can get my hands on! Be safe though; don't put yourself at risk by lying on tables that will collapse or anything else that might not go according to plan...

- Sets mean the exercise you are doing. So if I say do three sets of twenty push-ups, this means you need to perform twenty push-ups (set 1), take a break, do another twenty (set 2), break and then your final twenty (set 3).

- The icon > means you move from one exercise directly in to the next without any rest at all. Essentially the two exercises are linked and considered one set.

- If you're still unsure how to perform the exercises after reading my explanations below then I suggest you look them up on YouTube for further demonstration.

- This is only one example of how to use the pull up station to complete your workout. Once you've mastered this one then you can look to change your entire routine. Try researching other exercises online that you can perform at home. Ideally you should change your routine every six to eight weeks.

I have to assume that some of you reading this book have never exercised before; hence I've offered the detailed descriptions below. By the time we've finished this section you'll be able to understand why I'm only offering a few examples in this book as this is going to take quite a while!

And for the ladies reading this, if the exercises described seem a tad 'masculine' then don't worry, just keep reading and we'll get to the exercises more in line with your expectations.

Now let's look at each exercise in turn –

Push-ups

Is it safe to assume that everyone knows what a push-up is? I hope so or we're off to a really bad start! Just in case, I'll add one photo which, if anything, is surely overkill:

Actually one useful piece of information I can add is I like to vary the type of push-ups I do. These include standard push-ups (as seen above), wide arm, narrow grip, military, incline and decline push-ups. If you don't know what these are then just take a look online.

Crunches

Place your fingertips behind your ears, do not put your hands behind your head else you may pull on your neck and cause injury. Lie flat on your back with your knees up and use your abdominal muscles (abs) to pull your body up to a crunch position. You can increase the intensity of the exercise by extending your legs slightly as your body declines, then pull them back in towards your core as your body raises – open up your entire body, and then close in to a crunch.

Leg lifts

Keep your back flat. With straight legs, raise your feet a few inches off the floor. Raise your legs vertically and then lower your legs again. Don't allow your feet to touch the floor. If you want to make it harder then hold a weight with straight arms (don't move your arms as part of the exercise):

Station sit-ups

Now, I've called this 'station sit-ups' purely on the basis that the routine was built around the routine for James on the pull-up station. In reality, this is just a basic or 'classic' sit-up. You can do this with your feet locked under anything that will hold you in position. With your feet now in position, place your fingertips behind your ears (or better, fold them over your chest). Pulling from your abs, raise up and down under control. If you're doing this on carpet then watch out for carpet burns! I've learned this the hard way; I now sit on a pillow to avoid that painful friction!

V-sits

As per the picture, lay flat with your arms above your head. Then raise your body and legs together to form a 'v.' Make it harder by holding a weight in your hands.

Kettle bell squats

Lock the weight in to your chest. Place your feet shoulder width apart. Now sit in to the exercise. Push out your bum to protect your back – as per the picture.

Scissor lunges

Okay, you may have to YouTube this one as it's both hard to explain and a hard exercise to perform – I'll do my best with the explanation, you'll have to keep practicing until you get the hang of it. As per the start picture, place your body in a lunge position. Then, jump in to the end photo. This means you're jumping from one lunge position in to the next, Make sense? Do this for twenty reps (ten on each leg).

Wide reverse grip pull-ups

And as I'll maintain throughout, these upper body exercises are absolutely not limited to just the boys routines:

With your palms pointing away from you and your arms as wide as you can go, raise yourself up and down under control (the decline is just as important as the incline so always control the entire exercise). This is arguably the best upper body exercise you can do. It's also very hard so don't be put off if you can't do any at first. I suggest you jump to get yourself up and then control your body as you lower down. This action ultimately will improve your strength and allow you, in time, to pull yourself up.

Station vertical leg raises

On your pull-up station hold your body up with your arms. Keep your legs straight and raise them up and down under control. **Always** perform the exercises under control – no swinging your legs!

Narrow reverse grip pull-ups

This is essentially the same exercise as you performed for the wide grip version (you're now targeting different muscle groups and 'tweaking' the exercise). Aim to place your hands directly above your shoulders.

Station knee raises

This again is essentially the same as the station vertical leg raises you performed before. This time start with your legs straight, then raise your knees to your chest and repeat.

Now if you don't have access to this piece of equipment, or you want to tackle the more advanced version of this exercise, you might want to try hanging without a backrest (as ably demonstrated by Mirella Ingamells). Bear in mind you will need a strong core to hold yourself in position and not just end up swinging back and forth:

Pull-ups

Yet more pull-ups I'm afraid! With each exercise you'll be targeting different muscle groups so just keep on going. This time place your hands so your palms are facing toward you…and then start lifting.

Lying leg raise with vertical lift

In the picture you'll see our model, Scott, lying on a bench. This is great, however if you don't have a bench then you can perform the same exercise by lying on the floor with your hands on the floor by your side, across your chest, or better, holding out a weight above your head (such as in the v-sit position). It's similar to the leg lifts you performed in the morning. However this time when your legs are in the vertical position, raise your feet higher in to the air. Reverse the process by lowering your body and then your legs back to the floor. Remember to keep your ankles a few inches off the ground and don't put your feet down.

Kettle bell lunges

There's lots of different ways you can do this – with a single weight held at your chest, with a weight in either hand by your waist, with a bar over your shoulders, with no weight, and any other variant you can come up with yourself! Hold the weight and step forward into the lunge position, stand back up and repeat on the alternate leg. You should be aiming to have your knee (rear leg) touch the floor as you go down. Practice this without weight first and when you have the hang of it, use the weight(s) – as always we don't want to risk injuries.

Jumping squats

This is very simple. Here you start in the squat position and then jump up as high as you can (watch your head on the ceiling if working out at home!). As you land go straight back in to the squat position and repeat the process. Remember to sit in to the exercise in order to protect your back. Push up through the heels of your feet rather than your toes. If you want to make this exercise harder, you can start jumping on to something, such as a bench (the bench version is discussed later).

Station dips

Using the dip bars, start in an upright position with your arms locked out, then lower yourself down until your hands are under your armpits. As with pull-ups, you might not be able to do this exercise at first. Now don't panic, simply use your feet to push up from the floor and then slowly lower your body down. Again, your strength will soon build so you can perform the whole action. Also, rather than lowering yourself in a vertical position (which mostly will concentrate the exercise in your arms and shoulders), try to lean slightly forward (as per the diagram) as this will also target your chest.

Core pole twists

Take your pole, broom handle or whatever you're using and then twist from your hips from one side to the other. Twisting left constitutes one rep, twisting then to the right is two, and so on.

Station push-ups

Use the bars on your pull-up station to perform your push-ups. Keep your back straight and your core engaged (pull in your stomach and keep it tight). Again, I've named these 'station push-ups' as I would normally use my home equipment on the pull-up station. However as per the picture above, you could use push-up handles instead, and if you don't have those then just do push-ups! This is just a tweak and anything will do!

Van Dammes

Years ago I saw an interview with Jean Claude Van Damme where he was asked to explain how he came to have such a nice bottom. He explained he took the exercise from Kylie Minogue, who is also famous for having a lovely little bum. I was inclined to agree that both had well shaped rumps, thus 'Van Dammes' were firmly fixed in my mind forever!

Start by lying flat on the floor with your knees bent as seen in the diagram above. Put your hands wherever they're comfortable – on your chest or on the floor is fine. Now raise your hips and clench your buttocks as tight as you can and hold for three seconds. Lower your bum down to the floor and then repeat. Soon you'll have buns of steel!

Single leg bench lunge kettle bell touchdown

The name of this exercise is quite a mouthful and there's lots of different ways to do it, hence the need for two pictures this time. Ideally, you'll hold a kettle bell in each hand, or no weight if you want to make it a little easier. Place your rear leg on a bench, step, your sofa or whatever else you have at your disposal. With your weight on the front leg, lower your body down and touch the floor with your weights (or as close as you can get). You'll be using that front leg to lower down (under control) and then lift yourself back up again. Perform ten reps on the first leg and then swap. As I said earlier, you can make this easier by not using any weight.

Wood cutters

This is a great exercise for your core – targeting your abs and obliques. With your feet placed shoulder width apart and body facing forward, lift the weight over your shoulder. Twisting through the hips, drive the weight down across your body. Imagine you're holding an axe and chopping away at a tree. You need to keep a tight hold of the weight as you'll be driving down the weight with as much force as you can safely manage. I suggest you build up slowly with this exercise or you could risk an injury. The idea is to swing the weight down as hard as you can, as it gets to the bottom of your hip then fight against the momentum of the weight to stop it swinging any further. You should feel your core tighten with the effort. Perform ten reps on one side and then repeat on the other side.

Core wheel extensions

This is an advanced version of the Plank:

If you don't have a wheel or want to start with the easier version, then just plank. To do this put yourself in the push-up position but rest on your elbows. The most important thing to remember is to keep your back straight and core engaged (belly pulled in and tight) – if you don't then you're wasting your time. Hold this position for as long as you can.

If you're going to use the wheel then perform the same kind of action as the basic plank, although this time roll yourself back and forward on the wheel. This is a great exercise which you'll feel particularly through your shoulders and core.

And that brings us to the end of explaining how to perform that routine…now get to it! Before this chapter is complete, I'll share with you the full routine I performed to achieve my transformation.

Now before we go any further, let me address the question that will be crucial to many of you:

Can women train the same way as men?

The answer to this, somewhat surprisingly, is **yes**. Over the years I've had many ladies come to me with a request to write them a programme to get in shape. I always shied away from doing this as I was concerned it would result in their building arms as big as mine –

which clearly they didn't want. I've since learned the error of my ways. I now train alongside women at my gym, some of which are in there training just as hard as I am and doing basically the same routines. I've never been one for finding female bodybuilders attractive. Hey, we all like different things, girls with bigger muscles than me just doesn't flick my switch. But the girls in my gym today…phwoaarrrrrr! They have lean, toned, athletic bodies. When I go in to the gym I'm focused and not interested in the people around me, but the sight of these ladies tends to make me a tad more 'chatty' than I otherwise might have been!

Let's take a look at Louise doing her thing with a sledge hammer and a tyre:

Pretty darn hot right? At the time these were taken, she was training hard on a regular basis, hence being as toned as she is. You've already seen photos of Louise on nights on the town so we've demonstrated she still looks entirely feminine (and super-hot) with no sign of giant muscles.

Whilst I now have a far deeper knowledge of how women can (and should) train to achieve the type of results exhibited by Louise, I referred back to the experts (in this case Jason who trains women on a daily basis – and his clients are hot, hot, HOT!), for the scientific definition. Essentially it is as follows:

The answer is in testosterone and how it affects our bodies. Testosterone plays a major part in protein synthesis, which in turn is responsible for muscle recovery and therefore growth. Females produce around thirty times less testosterone than their male counterparts. This means then it is significantly harder for females to produce muscle growth than men. Now, if a woman was to engage in hypertrophy style training (three to four sets of eight to twelve reps), then growth will occur. However, the growth achieved will be significantly less than seen in a man training at the same level – relative to load and fatigue level – or will take considerably more effort than is required by men who naturally produce more testosterone.

So, to summarise or more accurately, translate that lot to English! Ladies, don't be afraid of picking up weights and don't think you can only lift small weights (with a higher number of reps) for fear that the big weights will make you look like men. Unless you start injecting yourself with testosterone, it is scientifically improbable that you'll build large, heavy muscle. What you will do over time is develop lean, sculpted and sexy muscle.

But as always, talk is cheap, let's back up the statements with some photo evidence. Gina, age thirty-three (left), and Selina, age forty (right), are friends of mine. Both use weights as their primary form of exercise, albeit it at different levels of intensity in order to achieve the bodies they want. Both have had children and are still able to rock hot little bod's that'll turn heads at the pool…

Still not 100% convinced? No, neither would I be, at least not without being offered more avenues to do my own research and more photographic evidence to support such bold and important claims. So, let's get serious now…and meet Mirella:

In order to properly introduce Mirella Ingamells (nee Clark), I should direct you to her website: mirellafitness.com. As always I must maintain that there's a great deal of information available out there, one of the key objectives of this book is to help you find the best sources and steer you away from gimmicks and fads. Mirella is far from a gimmick and her knowledge on the Health & Fitness industry far surpasses my own. I would strongly recommend you take the time to visit her website and investigate for yourself just what benefits you could take from the services she offers. You'll not be alone, even I shall be turning to Mirella for this very reason in the future…but more to follow on that in a future book!

As a very basic overview of Mirella's career history, Mirella became a Personal Trainer in her late twenties, some years on she is now a highly skilled and advanced industry subject matter expert. Mirella has worked in industry leading gyms and various countries including the UK, Abu Dhabi, and she is now based in Spain. Her wide and diverse client lists from around the world have even included a foreign Royal Family where she was assigned to a princess - pretty cool, huh?

Let me now share with you a quote from Mirella's personal mission statement which speaks to me at a personal level and is very much in keeping with the theme of this book:

"Health and fitness for me is a lifestyle choice. It's important for me to walk the walk and talk the talk. The industry is ever-evolving and I love to keep learning. Female strength and fat loss is where I like to focus most of my attention. I not only enjoy pushing clients beyond their limits, but the ultimate goal is to educate my clients, so that achieving better body composition becomes a lifestyle choice for the future, not just a 'fad diet' or an unsustainable unhealthy mission to get a 'bikini body'."

Finally and arguably the most impressive feather in her cap, Mirella is a champion in the leagues of The WBFF Diva Fitness and has competed on numerous occasions on their stages in the Diva Fitness Model category. Having won at the European Championship in 2013 (during her debut!), she then competed twice in the WBFF World Championships in Las Vegas. In 2013 she placed 3rd, and the following year took 2nd place. Very impressive Mirella, bravo!

Here's a quick look at Mirella in competition mode:

As you can see, Mirella is no stranger to the gym! I should note that Mirella and I have not consulted regarding diet and training programmes; Mirella's will be quite different from that I've set out in this book. As I've continuously stated, this book is not designed to get you 'stage ready,' it's purely focused on a balanced, healthy and sustainable model for the masses. However what we can see here ladies is even when you take your training to the upper levels of the spectrum, you can achieve incredible results without the risk of bulking up or becoming a tank!

Now of course I do appreciate that not all ladies reading this book will have aspirations to take their training to the same extremes as Mirella and ultimately achieve the same degree of muscularity. However let me make a very important distinction now, in order to step out on stage Mirella does have to go through an awful lot of preparation, both in her training regime and in her diet. We can see from the picture below that her body looks very different during the periods leading up to a competition to how it does for the majority of the year:

So whilst not every girl would want to sport the same kind of eight-pack as Mirella at competition time, I'm sure that a great many would kill for a body like hers when she's not in 'hardcore mode.'

But remember, the point of this section is to accurately demonstrate the fact that women can train properly with weights alongside the men. So whilst Mirella spends a significant amount of time in the gym doing this:

She can still head out on the town in a little dress without fear of being mistaken for a man and looking like this:

Again, if that's not hot then I don't want to know what is!

Still not convinced? Oh come on ladies, how much more proof do you need?! Okay, well Mirella has very kindly assisted me here by asking a handful of her clients to come forward and share their transformation pictures. Seriously, go and have a look on her site for other examples, some of them are absolutely amazing! To be totally honest and blunt, for the majority they start at a position where I wouldn't look twice at them in a bar…now that their transformations are complete I find myself offering Mirella the keys to my house and handing over my bank details just to get their phone numbers! Ha, and if I'm really honest then probably any of them would do as they all look that good!

The following examples are all of ladies who have competed on stage – I thought that would be a nice way to demonstrate their progress. Here we'll see their starting point next to a progress shot, and finishing in peak condition on stage. Of course Mirella trains female (and male) clients of all levels ranging from those that want to complete a transformation attune to my own; right up to those industry professionals who want to take their routines to the next level and win in competitions. Anyway, enough waffle, on to the girls…

Davina – age 27:

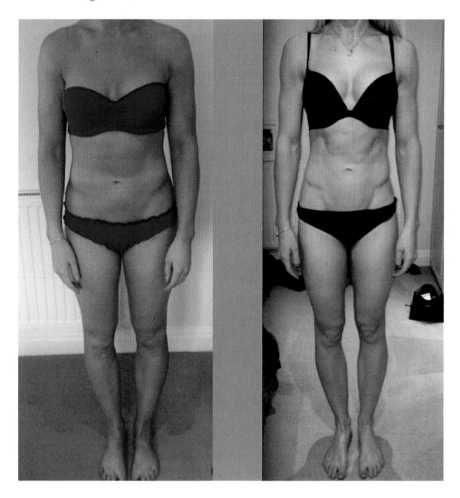

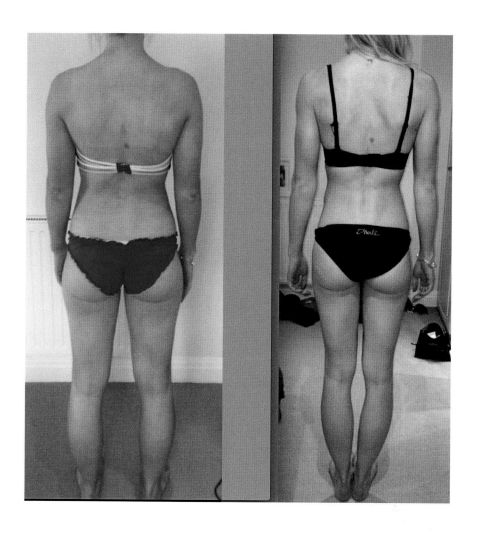

Lauren – age 31:

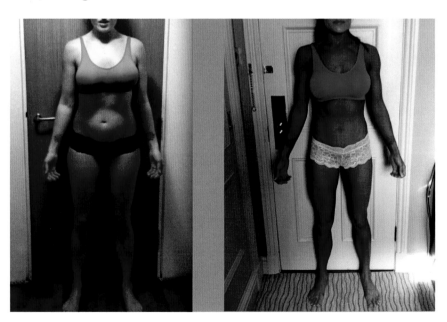

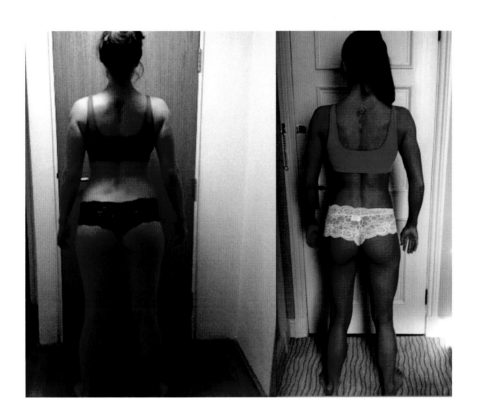

Kitti – age 28:

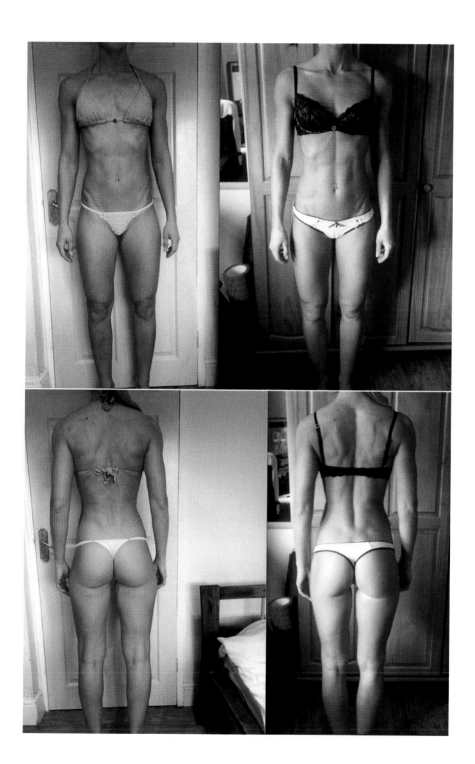

Stacy – age 31:

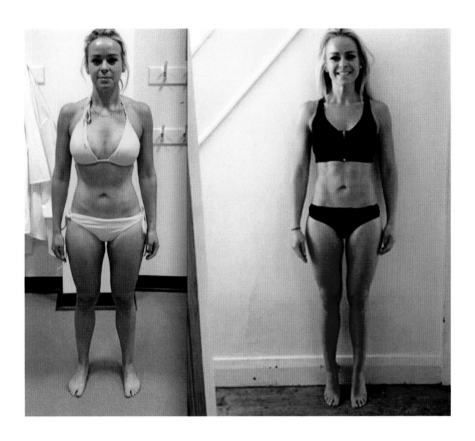

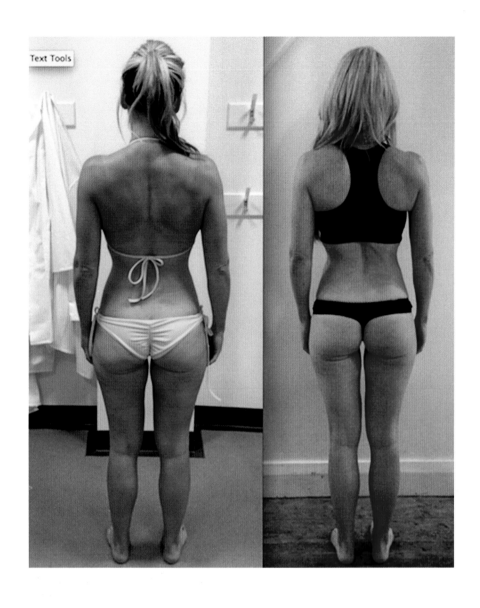

Let me make on important clarification at this stage: Remember the point I'm demonstrating. I've chosen to show you these girls to prove that ladies can train hard using weights without losing their feminine figures, I'm not showing you these to demonstrate transformations attune to my own. It's likely that some of you reading this will think our models have achieved muscularity levels beyond what you want to. However, do remember the crucial point that they've trained specifically for competitions. During this time they'll be eating around eight times per day, taking enough muscle building supplements to fund a small chemist for a year, and are training to levels that even surpass my own regime. Despite these facts, they're still not going to be mistaken for men in drag…in my opinion they're very firmly in the 'hot chick' category.

Point proven yet? I'd say yes. Let's close out this point with a picture of Sharon (one of Jason's many female clients) who is far from messing around with the dinky weights. Sharon is aged thirty-three and a mother of two children – you won't hear her making excuses that pregnancy has ruined her body and there's no way to get rid of the baby weight! Here we find her deadlifting an olympic bar with 25kg plates on either side (I know men that can't manage that!):

…and Mirella doing the same:

So ladies, before you head in to the gym and hop on the bench press, ask yourself what areas of your body actually need the most work. Now don't get me wrong, I think the entire body should have the same level of focus. Of course I am a guy so am guilty as the next person of this. I'll spend three to four days of the week working on my upper body, and only one on my legs. I use the rationale that I use my legs in other areas, such as running, but ultimately I'm just not as interested – chicks dig big chests and shoulders! My legs are big enough to match my upper body, just without quite so much development and/or definition. So if the men want to attract a female with their broad shoulders and bulging biceps, I've typically found that ladies want to focus on areas of their bodies more appealing to a man...so legs, bums and tums it is then. To summarise my point, if you look at James' routine, this is very focused on developing the upper body. Yes, you should still perform the same type of exercises, however rather than doing a total of nine sets of pull-ups (as per the main routine – and bearing in mind James was set to do this routine five days per week), which targets your arms, shoulders, back, etc., why not choose to maximize your routine in the areas where you're most focused? You should, of course, incorporate the upper body pull-ups, however perhaps don't make them the main attraction of the workout.

I knew a lady who was naturally petite and very small in the waist. She typically carried her fat (which relatively speaking wasn't much) in her thighs, bum and upper arms (close to her armpits). She wasn't a huge fan of the gym and had a very busy work/life schedule. Nonetheless she asked me to write her training programme for her. We agreed she could manage three hours per week (which is hardly excessive) and in addition would exercise by doing things she had a natural interest in, such as walking, yoga and horse riding. This seemed like a fair compromise to me. For my end of the bargain, I provided the following routine which was intended to be very high intensity (thus burning off that flab) and toning up her muscles, particularly in her trouble spots:

Day 1:

- 3 x Sets bench jump squat (10 x reps) > forward/reverse weighted lunge (total 4 x steps)
- 3 x Sets smith machine box squats (10 x reps) > scissor lunges (16 x reps)

- 3 x Sets leg extension (18 x reps) > core cable twists (8 x reps each side)
- 3 x Sets jump kettle bell squats (10 x reps) > cable core sword parry (12 x reps each side)
- 3 x Sets leg press (18 x reps) > cable core punch (12 x reps each side)
- 2000 meter row (best effort)

Day 2:

- 40 x Minute treadmill (constant pace) > 10 x minute cool down walk
- 3 x Sets dead lift shoulder press (12 x reps)

Day 3:

- 3 x Sets reverse grip pull-ups (10 x reps)
- 3 x Sets pull-ups (10 x reps)
- 3 x Sets decline push-ups (max effort to failure) > incline push-ups (max effort to failure) > kettle bell swings (10 x reps)
- 3 Sets thigh crunchers (15 x reps) > reverse thigh crunchers (15 x reps)
- 3 x Sets Arnold press (10 x reps) > weighted v-sits (12 x reps)
- Sprint interval training (2 x minute warm up, 6 x minute sprints)

Now to explain these exercises. You'll note that some of the exercises are repeats of those already documented in James' routine, so refer back to that section for the explanation. As before, if you're still unsure of how to perform the exercise then I suggest you look on YouTube for a demonstration video.

As always, don't be put off if you can't do the number of reps I've set out for this programme. Start off slowly if needed and gradually build up – both in the number of reps and the speed at which you work through the routine. We're super-setting at quite an intense (and advanced) level; even fit people will find this one tough, so ease yourself in. Again with the pull-ups, if you can't do them yet then as always, don't be put off, simply jump up (rather than pulling yourself up) and lower yourself down under control. Soon enough you'll be able to perform the exercise. Always remember, I find the only way to get good at pull-ups…is to do pull-ups!

And very importantly, also don't forget the > icon means you move directly on to the next exercise with no break!

Bench jump squat

Start in a squat position (sitting deep and pushing out your bum to take the pressure off your back). Then jump on to a bench, box, or whatever you are using. Jump backward off the bench and land in the squat position, then repeat.
If, when you're starting out, you find this a touch too intense, then jump on to the bench and then step down. As you get fitter you can jump on and off the bench.

Forward/reverse weighted lunge (total 4 x steps)

You learned earlier how to perform a lunge. This time you'll walk forward taking two lunges, and then walk backwards in a reverse lunge motion for another two steps. If you want to make it harder then hold a weight across your chest, or kettle bells in each hand, or a bar across your shoulders (so many fun options!).

Smith machine box squats

There are so many different ways to perform a squat – you've already seen examples in James' routine, and above you'll see Mirella demonstrating a classic squat. So if you don't have access to a Smith Machine, then don't worry. I like using the Smith as I suffer slightly with a bad back; this equipment helps protect it. Rather than standing in a conventional squat position, place your feet much further forward than normal. This will again protect your back and target different muscle groups not worked during other squat exercises. This may not feel natural at first but don't worry, the bar you're holding on the Smith Machine will keep you balanced (obviously you can only position your feet like this when using a Smith). Now, squat down much farther than normal, almost to the floor – it helps to put a small box under you, that way you know when your bum touches it then it's time to come up again. I realise this might seem obvious but this is a hard exercise and you'll want to cheat! Having to touch the box with your bum will keep you honest! Control everything from your legs and scream/grunt (or use a lot of profanity) to get yourself through this one!

Leg extension

This one is nice and easy as you'll be using the leg extension machine – it only works one way so you can't go wrong.

Core cable twists (8 x reps each side)

I love these core exercises using the cable pull, they work your abs and do a wonderful job on your obliques – let's get rid of those nasty love handles. Again, there are lots of different ways to perform the exercise, really there's no right or wrong answer. Personally I like the version demonstrated by the guy. I stand facing the cable machine, far away enough that the weight is held taught. With straight arms, twist from the hips as far as you can go, hold for one second and then return to the centre. Now twist the other way, repeating the previous action, and then return to the centre. Complete a total of sixteen twists.

Kettle bell jump squats

You've already seen this exercise in various other forms throughout this chapter, thus it shouldn't need any further explanation. Do remember to touch the weight to the floor and aim to jump as high as you can.

Cable core sword parry

Is this the accurate name for this exercise? Ha, probably not! It's what I call it as I imagine myself wielding a sword and parrying a blow that is coming down from above my head. Still, someone else must have thought the same as when I Googled it the same exercise came up – great minds and all that jazz!

Position yourself side on to the cable machine, and hold the handle with both hands (set it low at the bottom of the machine). Twisting through the hips, raise the cable above your head and block that sword blow!

Leg Press

Here's another simple one to perform on a machine where it's really very hard to get it wrong. Plant your feet and just start pushing. If you put your toes on the bottom of the foot rest then you can raise yourself up and down to work your calves, a great way to max out this set.

Cable core punch

Here's your final core exercise on the cable machine. This time have your back to the machine (side on as demonstrated by Scott is also fine) with the cable set around shoulder height. Grasp the handle with one hand and rotate through the hips for a punch movement (under control as always). Remember, the effort is made through your core; you're not pulling the weight from your shoulder.

Dead lift shoulder press

If it wasn't for the fact that this is just about my favourite exercise, then I wouldn't have included it in this book – it's going to be a complete pain to have to explain! You can perform the exercise using dumb bells or kettle bells; I like to do it with the bar. It is essentially the action of picking up your weight from the floor, lifting it up past your body, pressing it over your head, and finally controlling the descent until it's back on the floor again. I like this exercise as you're pretty much working all your body in one go. Also, having spent forty minutes running on a treadmill you should already be pretty tired. I keep the weight on this exercise quite low and pump through the reps to keep my heart rate up. By the end of the third set I'm breathing just as hard as I was on the treadmill – a fantastic way to finish off the session!

Let's break this exercise down into its key stages:

As stated, start with the weight on the floor and squat down to pick it up. Remember to have your feet flat on the floor and push through the balls of your feet rather than your toes. As you stand up, focus on lifting the weight through your legs. Your back will naturally be engaged, there is a tendency to allow your back to do all the work, thus focus on your legs so they take more of the strain.

Lift the bar up from your waist to your shoulders in one jerking movement to position for the press phase.

Now press the bar above your head. As you start to tire and can't press it anymore, it's okay to cheat and bend your knees for that added momentum. Until that time, keep your legs straight and press through your shoulders. Now lower the bar down to your chest.

Rotate your arms to allow the bar to return to your waist. As you do this action, control the weight through your traps (your shoulders) - you should feel your traps tighten under the strain as your hands flip over (from palms facing up to palms facing down).

Squat back down to put the bar on the floor and repeat.

It sounds complicated but really isn't that hard! Just pick up the bar and figure it out.

Decline push-ups

It's as simple as it looks. With your feet on a bench, perform your push-ups and keep going until you can't do any more.

Incline push-ups

Now reverse the exercise.

Kettle bell swings

The key to this exercise is to let the weight swing. All the effort comes from your legs; you shouldn't use your arms at all. From the start position push up through your legs and allow the momentum of the weight to swing your arms forward. As the weight starts to fall, bend your knees and allow the weight to return to the start position, then repeat.

Thigh crunchers

Using this machine, start with your legs nice and wide and then close for a crunch. I've only ever seen women performing this exercise in gyms; I personally like to do it myself. Hey, why wouldn't I want nice shapely inner thighs?

Reverse thigh crunchers

Now reverse the setting on the machine and go again.

Arnold press

Devised by Arnold Schwarzenegger himself (hence the name), this is just an amazing exercise to hit your chest, shoulders and arms all in one go.

Start with the weight at your chest, with your fingers facing toward you. Now press the weight above your head, twisting your arms on the way up so your fingers end up facing away from you. Twist again on the way back down to your chest and return to the start position.

Sprint interval training

On the treadmill, start by walking and gradually increase the speed to a jogging pace over the space of around two minutes. Now increase the speed to your sprint pace and run as fast as you can, for as long as you can. When you can't run any more, put your feet to the side and rest for fifteen seconds. Be strict with yourself, as soon as fifteen seconds has elapsed, jump back on and keep sprinting. Keep doing this until your set time has finished. I normally sprint for around six to eight minutes – for me that's more than enough, especially considering my weight routine has been very intense with little rest (and thus becoming a cardio workout as much as a weight routine).

So, that covers the section devoted to our lady readers. Guys, don't think you can't use this routine yourselves, the point I've stressed is the exercises are all the same, just do a little more for the areas you're most interested in.

Now let's look at this chapter's 'Top Tips:'

- If you're smiling, chatting or otherwise happy when training, then something is going seriously wrong. This is the level you need to train to

This photo isn't staged, it's the end of a very hard session and I've literally collapsed…much to the delight of a triumphant Scott!

- Weights are the foundation of my regimen; however I need a more rounded routine. I must include interval training, distance running, sports (mostly playing squash), swimming and gym classes, e.g. spinning. Whatever kind of training regimen you plan for yourself, it's best to mix things up and add in other activities to complete your overall routine.

- I don't want to sound like a broken record here…but if you're going to follow my advice and train with weights, then get that intensity as high as you can manage. As per the examples you've already seen, supersets are a really great (and basic) way to do this. You can experiment with your supersets by combining two, three or even four different exercises as one set. The beauty of training this way is your weight sessions will become cardio sessions so you'll burn blubber whilst sculpting sexy muscles. Winner!

- No matter what your body shape or what you've done in the past, there's always a way to change – **always.** When I was twenty-one, I weighed 13 stone (82kg/182lbs). I trained regularly in a style not too dissimilar to how I train today. I looked like this:

- By the time I was twenty-nine I weighed 16.5 stone (105kg/231lbs). I'd started training differently; I was focused more on heavy weights and did hardly any cardio. This led to me looking like this:

Although I enjoyed being big and strong, I personally have always preferred to have a more athletic apperance. Even when I started to train again as I did in my younger years, nothing changed. At that time I thought it was just a symptom of my age and I'd forever be big no matter what I did. I know now that this is due to my not having changed my diet, **I needed to fast (through juicing) to burn off all that excess weight and effectively reset my body.** At the time I continued eating as I'd always done. Actually when I was younger I ate a lot of bad foods, however I was able to maintain an attractive body because of the way I trained, but also because I had the benefit of youth on my side.

Obviously, as we age, our bodies can't stand the same level of abuse. I said previously that it's possible to look great on the outside whilst being unhealhy on the inside. In addition to not consumming enough vegetables (particularly in their raw natural state), I was poisoning myself with a constant supply of processed foods, particularly chocolate and ice cream. There was a stage in my life where I was addicted to Ben & Jerry's Chocolate Fudge Brownie ice cream. I'd eat one or sometimes even two large tubs per day! I was training around four hours per day (I certainly don't have time to do that any more!), so still looked good.

Fast forward a few years to my early thirties. Now I found myself in a position where I'd not trained in years and had swapped most of my muscle for fat. I weighed the same 16.5 stone as I did when I was bulked up with heavy muscle. Remember, muscle weighs more than fat so it goes to show just how much fat I'd put on. I looked, as you know by now, like this:

Again, I convinced myself that there was no way back. I'd tried occasional bouts of training under my old gym regime and tried eating less food. I'd never see any significant results so would always give up.

Of course having now reset my body through my new diet and having redesigned my training regimen, I was proven completely wrong. **<u>There is always a way to change how you look</u>**. Fifteen years later I again am sporting a body more in keeping with the physique I liked so much in my early twenties:

These days I weigh in around 14 stone (90kg/198lbs). When I went to Las Vegas I was slightly heavier as I was training harder and was therefore more muscular. Despite being a stone heavier than the photo you saw when I was twenty-one; I'd say I'm close to being as lean. And if nothing else, I'm far from where I was less than a year ago:

Now you've seen proof that change can be made, you surely can have no more excuses!

- So what about 'muscle memory?' There are various meanings of this term, in this example some people use it to say that once you have built muscle then it never goes away. Some of you might then think this is how I managed to get back in to good shape so quickly. Whilst there is some truth to this, be under no illusion that I had to work extremely hard. When I was in my early to mid-twenties I could take a break from the gym for a few months. If I then trained hard for two weeks it would be as though I hadn't so much as missed a day. That was a wonderful time! However, having had six years of not training my muscles had shrunk, were weak and generally had to be totally rebuilt.

- Here's a big one for the list of top tips…**say no to drugs!** I'm confident that at least one reader of this book will achieve fantastic results and be tempted then, at some stage, to push their training to the next level. Yes, take steroids and you will achieve results way beyond those you can achieve naturally. Bear in mind though, **using steroids is dangerous**. When I was younger we all joked that we didn't want to do steroids for fear that it might shrink our 'gentleman parts,' one of the reported side effects of steroid use. Now I'm older I've seen countless examples of some of my childhood heroes either suffering with heart conditions, or otherwise dying young of sudden heart attacks. As two prime examples, Arnold Schwarzenegger's heart attack was rumoured to be the result of his steroid use. I personally haven't read anything that confirms this but I'd be surprised if it's not the case. Another of my favourites as a boy was the WWF wrestler, The Ultimate Warrior – a hugely muscular guy who abused steroids for decades. He dropped dead aged fifty-four in 2014. Actually I understand this to be very common in professional wrestling which has a disproportionately high number of athletes who die prematurely, many of which are linked to drugs and steroids.

I know a guy who has been using steroids for a short period of time (perhaps for a couple of years). He told me that following a recent visit to the doctor he was told that his blood pressure was high and his heart was edging towards being of an abnormal size. Remember, your heart is a muscle and like the rest of you, it will grow. If you're exercising then your heart is also getting a workout, it stands to reason then, that it can grow. Well that's my interpretation at least! Right or wrong just keep it simple and stay off the hard stuff. Even I am tempted on occasion. I know a group of guys who are regular users, their bodies are, well, perfect. Being fantastic as opposed to perfect is a small price to pay for not risking a premature death!

- Some say that if you've got weight to lose then you should start with cardio to lose it, and then pick up the weights to build the body you're after. Anyone who tells you this is a fool! I learned very early on that the best way to lose weight is to train with weights (I suppose the clue then is in the title!). During some of those periods in my younger life when I'd fallen off the wagon and gained some fat, I tried going back to the gym and running – mostly longer runs between thirty to sixty minutes. After two weeks I'd still show very little sign of improvement. However on the occasions where I'd go straight back to lifting weights, two weeks later I'd look as though I'd never stopped training and any chub I'd gained would be gone.

Let me tell you a story about Mikey. Many years ago, Mikey started coming to the gym with me. Although we only trained together for around six months, whilst under my direction Mikey was in the best shape of his life (you'd think that would have given him some faith in my methods). Like me, Mikey stopped training and got fat, even fatter than me. Over the years Mikey has also made attempts to get back in shape, each time hiring Personal Trainers, each time failing to lose the weight. With these trainers he'd mostly focused on cardio without any real emphasis on weight training – I've told him each time this is **wrong**. Since my transformation, Mikey has returned to me and asked for my new secret. I gave Mikey instruction on how my diet works and told him to get back in the gym.

Unfortunately Mikey again hired himself a trainer who had him focused on cardio routines telling him to get his weight down and then start using weights. Now the good news is Mikey has lost a significant amount of weight. I'd attribute this to following my diet (to an extent at least, he certainly didn't follow it to the letter) and finally getting some much needed exercise. However he didn't come close to achieving the same results as I have. It's a great shame, because had Mikey just done what I told him to do and followed the same training routine as me (which is a cardio based weight routine), then by now he would have been ripped! I don't think Mikey keeps up with my diet plan much these days. He's once again fallen in to the trap of not seeing fast enough results, and has subsequently given up. If you're reading this Mikey, stop listening to these 'so called experts' and for once listen to me – I got you there once, I'll get you there again!

Now let me make a clarification. Obviously doing lots of cardio will help you to lose weight. If your goal is to burn off fat, then in my experience, and as previously stated, it will take that much longer than by weight training. However, cardio is the most effective way to burn off muscle, should the case be that you've found yourself getting a tad too big. During my basic training in the Army, I was subjected to countless hours of training, mostly in the form of long runs and high intensity circuit training sessions. I soon lost the majority of my muscle mass and was that much slimmer. I didn't notice it. I recall going home six weeks later for my first bout of leave and my girlfriend at the time looked at me like an AIDS victim – I think she called me 'gaunt,' or something to that effect! Remember what I've said; choose the training programme that suits the results you want to achieve. More proof that my statements are true are delivered by the Hollywood actor, Mark Wahlberg. I recently watched a trailer for his movie 'The Gambler.' In recent years he's been sporting quite a muscular physique; in this film I thought he looked oddly skinny. I then noticed in the trivia (as listed on IMDB.com), that in order to perform the role he'd lost 61lbs. How did he do it? That's right, by performing cardio workouts and living mostly on a liquid diet and eating vegetables. Well that's how they list it on IMDB, it clearly means he's been juicing…see, they're all at it!

So, do your weights and cardio to burn off the flab. If you feel like you're starting to get a bit too muscular then add more cardio to your routine. However if you train according to the style I've suggested (high intensity) then there shouldn't be any risk of you getting bulky.

- These days the experts are recommending we trade in our long 'steady state' cardio exercise for interval training. By steady state I mean we train at the same level for a given period of time. In English, that would be an example of your running on a treadmill at the same speed and on the same incline – let's say for thirty minutes. In the same example, interval training on a treadmill would be where you frequently change the speed and/or the incline. As I'm informed, the science states that after fifteen minutes your body adapts to what you're doing and you stop getting the full benefit of the exercise. If, however, you're constantly shocking your body by changing the exercise then you have to work significantly harder, forcing you to burn more calories.

So does this work? Actually, yes, it does. One of my oldest friends is called Dave – we spoke of him earlier as another no-nonsense Personal Trainer. Dave and I were both in the Army together and he's always been very serious about his fitness. However, he's naturally a big, barrel chested guy (very broad in the chest and sternum). In the old days we always used to exercise in our weights and cardio routines in that 'steady state' mode. Despite being muscular and extremely fit, Dave always carried a layer of fat, was never very well defined and if anything, he had a big old fat head and belly! Around three years ago Dave switched to the explosive routines I've described and replaced the long runs for interval training. At age forty-three, ironically he's now in better shape than when I first met him at age twenty-eight. Let's look at the results:

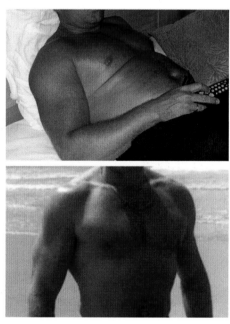

It's a shame Dave didn't want his face to be included as then you'd be able to see the chiselled jawline he now sports.

However, I'm not convinced there is no place left in my routine for those long, steady state cardio sessions. Have you ever seen a fat long distance runner? Me either, so it must be doing something good for us! I try to do a steady-state run around twice a week as part of my overall routine.

- In whatever exercise you're performing, form is everything. **Never compromise form.** I see it all the time when I go to the gym, particularly in young men full of testosterone wanting to show everyone else how much they can lift. Yes, I've been guilty of this on more than a few occasions! If you're lifting weights then it's better to lift a lighter weight which is under control at all times, rather than a heavier weight that you have to swing or jerk your body to shift. You may think it makes you look impressive, however those more experienced people you're trying to impress will just laugh, knowing it's too heavy for you. Worst of all, if you're not doing the exercise properly then you'll not be getting the full benefit for your effort...so you're wasting your time and effort – which is a total sin! These days I'm very happy to lift lighter weights, lift them properly and sport a better body for it. If you look better than the guys lifting heavier weights than you, then who's the real winner?

- I'm conscious that I may appear to have a poor opinion of Personal Trainers based on some of the comments I've made during the course of this book. This couldn't be further from the truth. I respect skilled and knowledgeable professionals no matter what their industry is. In Jason's case, I would happily let him talk at me for hours, lapping up all the knowledge he had to share. At various stages in my life I wanted to become a Personal Trainer (ultimately I decided a more formal career would be best). However, do bear in mind that you can become a certified Personal Trainer within a matter of weeks. If you're choosing to hire one as part of your transformation then do bear in mind that some are better than others, and it's always worth questioning what you're being told rather than blindly following instruction.

- I stated in the Diet Chapter that you should eat for your type, noting the differences between Scott's tall and naturally lean body, and my shorter and broader body. The same applies here, so train for your body type. If you're skinny and want to build muscle then you'll need to place more emphasis on lifting heavy weights than on your cardio (and of course eat more). If however you're of an average or heavy build then my explosive style routines should work best for you.

- People question how often you should train. I know people who train every day, I know others that train three days per week. I know some people who will train three times per day, I know others who train just once. **The key is finding what is right for you.** Our bodies are different and just as they will respond differently to food, they'll also respond differently to exercise. Over the years I have found that my best results come from training twice a day, five days per week. These days that constitutes about around forty-five to sixty minutes for my morning session, and around thirty to forty-five minutes in the afternoon/evening. When I was younger I averaged around four hours training per day (five days a week). However based on my new routine and having cut out the majority of the rest time, I can still squeeze almost as much into my current routine and achieve results as good as my younger days. Besides, I now have neither the time nor the inclination to be spending four hours per day in the gym!

On a similar topic, let's discuss the myth of 'over-training.' I've heard some say that you can't train for more than forty-five minutes per day; if you do it will have negative effects on your body. Well what an absolute load of nonsense! I'm convinced someone once said it as a joke and somehow it spread (probably amongst lazy people!). My answer to those people is always to go and speak to professional bodybuilders who spend hour after hour in the gym and are the size of buses. Tell them they're overtraining and see what reaction you get! Again, it's all about finding what the right amount is for you.

As much as you shouldn't be afraid to train hard and frequently, you've also got to take time to rest. Scott trains once a day, four days per week. I like to (if I can), train twice a day, five days per week. But we both take time off. Your body needs this time to recover and repair. I recall having to do a fitness test when I was going through my basic training in the army. I'd just returned from two weeks of leave (holiday/vacation) and was concerned that I hadn't trained so thought my results would be affected. As it turned out, I ran faster than ever. This was because my body had been rested and had time to fully recover, thus I'd returned fitter and stronger. As I stated earlier in the book, every couple of months or so I force myself to take a full week off – no healthy diet, no training. After a week of rest I look and feel better.

- As part of planning how you're going to exercise, consider also your abilities. If you have medical conditions then you'll need to consult with your doctor before embarking on a new strenuous regime. One of my friends suffered with problems with his hips meaning that he could no longer run – the impact of running was painful and aggravated it further. He might have chosen to stop exercising altogether. However he made the right choice and instead turned to cycling which didn't put the same impact on his hips.

- Exercising isn't only about the time you spend in the gym (or wherever you'll be training). You can make the conscious decision to get a bit more exercise throughout your day. If you find yourself waiting for the lift (elevator) to arrive, then why not take the stairs instead? If you need to pop out to your local shop for some milk, do you really need to drive or could you walk? I have a deep-rooted hatred for people who step on a travelator (such as you find in airports) and then immediately stop walking. Seriously, how lazy do you have to be to let something else walk for you? Okay, if you have an injury or medical condition whereby it's painful to walk then so be it, you're the exception to the rule. For everyone else, shame on you! The point is you can make tiny changes to most aspects of your day and continue burning those extra calories.

- You can always find time to train. As we discussed in the chapter on motivation, you need to plan when you'll be able to fit it in to your busy days. When I got fat, it was partly due to my never finding time to go to the gym. "I'll just finish off these last few emails, then I'll go to the gym at 7pm" I'd say. Of course before I knew it, it would be 10pm and exercise would be the last thing on my mind. These days I've accepted a work/life balance must exist, so insist on taking an hour for myself. If I'm really busy and can't get away, then I'll do some exercises in the office – do an email, then do some squats, do an email, then do some sit-ups. I realise this won't be suitable for everyone (it might look a little silly if you work in a crowded office and jump out of your booth for twenty star-jumps), but you can find your own way to fit it in.

- **Never** skip leg day! This probably won't be a concern for the majority of ladies reading this book; it's the men who are normally the guilty parties. Men typically aspire towards the hallowed six pack, big arms and chiselled chest. However, it's no good having a great upper body if your legs don't match. When I was younger I thought my legs were getting enough exercise through all the running I did, however even I started to develop the dreaded 'chicken leg' form. This had to change immediately! As irony would have it, my calves are now one of my best body parts – annoying as I'd rather have my best feature on my chest, stomach or one of the more important areas! Oh well, I suppose that's just the way it goes…

- Some trainers, including mine, will tell you not to overwork your abs. Jason made a very sensible statement one day to the effect of "You wouldn't train your chest every day would you?" Now I actually can't fault that logic at all. Another friend called Andy told me his trainer said you don't need to train abs at all. Despite his trainer having a body that really is ready for a bodybuilding stage, Andy follows this guidance and unsurprisingly has no sign of a six pack.

The best six-packs (or eight-packs) I've seen have been sported by those who do hundreds of sit-ups every day. The best six-pack I've ever had was therefore, unsurprisingly, when I was performing hundreds of sit-ups five days a week. Case in point, Jason's diet is pretty much perfect for building muscle (diet being essential if you want to create the perfect six-pack), and whilst he does have a very well defined stomach, his abs would be far better developed were he to spend more time doing his crunches.

If you want great abs, then spend plenty of time working on them. It's as simple as that.

- On a similar topic, the question exists of how often you should work on your arms (this one is probably more of interest to the guys). Note that if your goal is to build big arms then you should concentrate more on your triceps – the larger portion of your arm. I used to train my arms, specifically targeting my biceps and triceps for full sessions twice a week. I've since learned that this really isn't necessary. As you know, my routines change every six to eight weeks. For some of the routines I don't include any exercises designed for arms, e.g. bicep curls and tricep dips. For all your upper body routines, you'll be using your arms so they'll be getting a good workout without having to specifically target them. If you consider pull-ups as a prime example, there you'll work mostly on your arms whilst training your back and shoulders. Don't skip arms altogether, just aim to add them into other areas of your routine, perhaps a couple of bicep or tricep exercises on back day? You get the point.

- In terms of achieving definition, I've actually found in the past the best way to do this is not by using weights, it's actually through body resistance exercises, e.g. push-ups, pull-ups, and so on. This most likely is due to the fact that you can perform more reps under your own body weight (remember the rule of lighter weights and higher reps for definition?). Be sure to mix in your body resistance exercises with the weights.

- As you've seen for James' routine, I've set a number of reps for each exercise, i.e. <u>20</u> x push-ups followed by abs, then another <u>20</u> x push-ups, etc. A really good way to tweak your routine (for all exercise programmes) is to perform your reps to failure, i.e. keep performing the exercise until you can't do any more. When you're doing your first set it might feel like it's going on forever, however keep the intensity of your workout high with little rest. On the next two sets you'll find your muscles are completely fatigued so you're able to do significantly less. This is a great way to shock your system and will help transition you to the next stage in your physique and training levels.

- As I've already discussed, be prepared to start exercising at a low level. Yes, push yourself hard, but gradually increase the intensity. Don't worry, your body will tell you when you've had enough! Of course over time you will be able to push yourself harder and harder. This would be a good time to consider maintaining your body in other areas, such as having semi-regular sports massages. I pushed myself to breaking point over the four months leading up to my trip to Las Vegas without having any such support, or even making time to stretch before and after my workouts. A week before we flew I had terrible sciatica shooting down my leg and a sore lower back. Essentially my hamstrings had tightened almost to breaking point. The hamstrings lead to your lower back, hence my pain from my calf to my back. Now, I make sure I see my physiotherapist at least once a month to keep my body operational. I must warn you, a proper sports massage hurts like hell, but it's essential! Forget candles, spa music, hot oils and anything else you might be used to with your regular massage…

That should be more than enough to get you started and answer some of those all-important questions that might have come up. Now let's finish off this chapter with talking you through how I train – **finally!**

As I explained at the outset, I'm not going to provide you with my complete routine over the past year. It's changed several times and if you're new to the gym, then it will be overly complicated and advanced for you at this stage. I suggest then you research suitable exercises you can do for each body part (keep it simple) and work your way through the example routines below. Remember to change your routine every couple of months and consider tweaks that you can apply to continuously shock your system – perhaps lift heavier weights for one period to 'bulk,' then switch to lighter weights with higher reps to 'strip/cut.' Throw in occasional changes such as supersets or maximum efforts, or change some sets to four or even five (rather than the standard three sets), amongst many others. Don't worry, over time you'll learn all the tricks. But most importantly, keep your intensity high, reduce your rest time and push yourself **hard**! If you're not sweating and breathing heavily, well then you're not working hard enough.

When I was training at my peak I aimed to complete two sessions per day, five days per week. Each session would constitute around an hour. Some of you might be thinking that sounds a lot of effort, well then, consider that there are twenty-four hours in a day. If you're not overly active outside of your training then that's plenty of rest time! Of course life did often get in the way. Whilst the examples below are based on my optimum design, I probably only managed to do a second session around three times per week. So long as I continued to eat well and train at least once per day (during the week), then I didn't lose too much sleep over a missed second session here and there. Just do your best.

Example 1

For the main sessions (weight training), each time, select seven different exercises for that muscle group. Ensure the exercise is performed smoothly (no jerking) and under control at all times.

Monday

Main session:

Shoulders

Integrate a core routine with the seven different exercises. I suggest four exercises; you might want to use the cable core routine and woodcutters we previously discussed in this chapter. The core exercises should be completed as a superset to the shoulder exercise you are doing, i.e. as you finish your first set of dumb bell presses then move directly on to your first set of woodcutters with no rest, then immediately return to your second set of dumb bell presses, then immediately back to woodcutters, and so on. Finish the routine with sprints in the pool. Ideally aim to complete ten lengths of the pool. Sprint (your best effort) with the stroke of your choice (I do front crawl) down the pool, then sprint with another stroke (I then do breast stroke) back to the start point. Allow yourself a sixty second rest and then repeat.

Second session:

James' Main Routine

As I mentioned earlier, I'd already hit my cardio target for the day in my Main Session. Whilst I could have greatly increased the intensity of this second workout by cutting down the rest time, I'd invariably space it out over a period of about ninety minutes whilst watching a film. So, I'd do a set of pull-ups and then sit down to watch a bit of the film and have a rest. Whilst I may not have been maximizing the intensity values of the exercise, I was allowing myself the chance to do more reps (and therefore build more muscle) by taking it slower. Aside from that, I just didn't want to have to kill myself twice in the same day!

Tuesday

Main Session:

Back

This time, choose four different abs exercises to integrate and superset with your programme. Again, you may choose to select some of the examples I've set out in this chapter, e.g. crunches, V-sits, etc. Finish your session with a 2000 metre row (best effort).

Second Session:
Spin class
This is an intense workout which I highly enjoy and recommend. Previously I had shied away thinking it looked a bit too 'hardcore' for me and I didn't want to be embarrassed by not being able to keep up. The beauty of this is you can lower the difficulty setting on the bike so there's no reason why all can't do this one.

Wednesday
Main Session:
Legs
Choose four core or abs exercises to incorporate into your routine. You may choose a combination of the two. Finish the routine with a twenty minute run at a constant pace.

Second Session:
Insanity
As I mentioned earlier, I own the DVDs so would select one of the disks to do from home. Many gyms are now starting to offer Insanity classes, so it's more probable I'll choose to do the classes there in future.

Thursday
Main Session:
Chest routine
No abs on this occasion, I would extend the session slightly by either doing additional chest exercises (beyond the standard seven sets), or by adding a couple of exercises for biceps and/or triceps. Finish the routine with sprints (a two minute warm up followed by six to eight minutes of sprints).

Second Session:
A one hour game of squash followed by twenty minutes exercising on a cross trainer at a steady pace. This way I would benefit from the

short burst sprints on the squash court, and then shock my body with the steady-state exercise.

Friday
Main Session:
Cardio
A forty to sixty minute run at a constant pace. Follow this with either James' morning Routine, or a routine of deadlift shoulder presses supersetted with core exercises (three sets).

Second Session: None – it's now time for a well-deserved rest!

Example 2

This time I'll not list either the Second Sessions or the cardio exercise I'd perform to complete the Main Session. Invariably these would remain the same – so I'd always swim on a Monday to finish the Main Session and then complete James' Routine for my Second Session, etc. Note that some weeks it would vary, such as when I was travelling on business and therefore couldn't go for my spin class or play squash. In these cases I'd just do something else – normally running or using an exercise bike in the hotel gym.
Again, with this example, keep things simple at the start with performing three sets of ten reps for each exercise. As you learn more, you'll find ways to tweak the routine. Always end the session with some form of cardio (ideally sprint/interval training). And of course work on your abs and core for three days per week (not including the abs workouts you'll get in your second sessions).
For the most part, this is going to be a superset routine – as you've already learned, this means you'll go from one exercise directly in to the next.

Monday
Back & Shoulders
Choose six exercises for each body part. Start with your back and then superset into your shoulders. Finish the routine with one more exercise on each body part without a superset. So, it might look a bit like this –
- Undergrip row > standing dumbbell press

- Overgrip row > dumb bell shrugs
- D-grip bar row > dumbbell front raise
- Seated row > dumbbell side raise
- Lat pull-down > Arnold press
- Shoulder press machine
- Deadlift

Don't worry if you don't understand the exercises set out above, they're only offered to show you how the routine flows. Do not forget to mix in those abs/core exercises, so on some exercises you'll actually superset three different exercises together, e.g. lat pull-down > Arnold press > V-sits. You'll certainly get a sweat on with this one!

Tuesday
Biceps and triceps
Here you go; you've had a couple of months with the last routine with limited focus on your arms, now it's time to give them a bit more attention. As I said previously, you're always using your arms for the other exercises so don't think they're not getting bigger. This routine is more in line with 'stripping' (when you're cutting down your weight and aiming for greater definition) so it's timely to look to sculpt those arms into a lovely shape.

This time, choose only five exercises for your bi's and tri's, and superset between them (and add your abs!). This is more than enough for your arms.

As you're doing fewer exercises today this will leave you more time for cardio. Typically this is the day I'll do twenty to thirty minutes on the treadmill (steady state) at as fast a pace as I can manage.

Wednesday
Legs
Back to basics again with another routine of seven exercises which you'll superset. It's all legs so it might sound confusing when I say start with legs…and then go straight to legs. I'm sure you get the idea but just in case, here are a couple of examples:

- Leg press machine > calf extensions (on the leg press machine)
- Leg extension machine > scissor lunges

Do I need to remind you at this stage to mix in your abs and/or core? Hopefully not or else you've not being paying attention!

Thursday

<u>Chest</u>

Chest for the most part gets its own day because...well because it's awesome! Actually you get a pretty good shoulder and tricep workout when you do chest so you're going to leave the gym with great gains in other areas.

Again it's a case of choosing the seven supersets you want to do. A top tip is to not focus only on the classic 'push' exercises such as the bench press; you should also incorporate the 'pull' exercises – you'll do these mostly on cables. The pull exercises are brilliant for developing the shape of your chest.

So, a few quick examples:

- Bench press > push-ups (to failure)
- Incline bench press > decline push-ups (to failure)
- Cable flies > dumb bell flies

Friday

Provided you can still move by this stage, use this as a cardio day – much the same as we did in the first example.

Finally, that brings us to a close for this chapter. I confess, I had thought the diet chapter was going to be the longest one. Hey, I suppose the diet section isn't really that complex – juice, eat healthy unprocessed foods and have a treat here and there to enable the maintenance of your sanity. Simple really! Discussing how to train, particularly for those who might never have stepped foot in a gym, turned out to be slightly more of a challenge...

Chapter 6: What's Next?

Well firstly, my congratulations to you all for making it this far. You've finished the book and are now armed with the key information to get you started on your own transformation. Arguably this is actually where all the hard work begins, but stay focused and remember exactly why you're doing it:

You know the funny thing is, at the time the first photo was taken (during a skiing trip, hence the socks!), I'd lost some weight and actually thought I looked pretty darn good. Even funnier is, believe it or not, I'm actually flexing as hard as I can in that shot…whilst in the second I'm stood totally relaxed. Well, perhaps a bit more 'tautness' around the stomach but that's pretty standard!

In the immediate sense, what's next is you'll put down this book and head off to the supermarket to stock up on your healthy foods and then swing by your local gym on the way home. Fast forward a few months and you should be ready to send in your transformation photos. Come and find the From Fat to Fantastic page on Facebook. The best photos and stories will likely be included on the page and in the next book.

Not wishing to jump totally ahead of ourselves here – there's likely a long road ahead – but the day will come when like me, your transformation will be complete. Now we'll all react differently to this. Hopefully you'll take the sensible approach and keep going like me. However I have to be honest, even with another Vegas holiday booked I'm finding it hard to find quite the same level of focus as I did the first time round. Hey, I'm the lion on top of the mountain so now I'm not as hungry to climb to the top. I've thought about this long and hard and concluded I'm going to need a new challenge to throw myself in to…and lucky you, I intend to document it as a case study which shall be presented, that's right…in From Fat to Fantastic 2: Vegas Ready.

So here's an insight into what you can expect to find in From Fat to Fantastic 2 – Vegas Ready:

- As you know all too well by now, my diet plan is centred on health and moderation. I have no plan to ever deviate from this and will live by this mantra for the rest of my life. However, what about those occasions when you're on the countdown to your trip to Vegas (or beach holiday for you lesser mortals?) Perhaps then for a short period of time it would be acceptable to change up your routine for the sake of taking your body to the next level?
  Well this is precisely what I intend to explore. Yes, I'm delighted with the results I have achieved and have no shame by the pool, but what if I ate for the style of training I'm doing? What results would that bring? Well there's only one way to find out! So with four months to go, I'll be ditching my diet plan and accepting Jason's – he's been desperate for me to try this for the past year and I've finally given in for the

sake of science! Furthermore I'm going to follow his training regime to the letter…from what I've seen of it thus far, there's actually a lot more eating and less training involved – shocking? I'd say so! But hey, if I'm going to be able to accurately report the results back to you then I'm going to have to commit to it fully. Jason has promised to deliver the best version of my body I've ever seen…so fingers crossed! Like I've maintained throughout, you never stop learning so let's see what he has to offer…

- In order to document the process fully, I'll offer you a complete breakdown of the diet you'll need to follow, including delicious new recipes. Of course by this stage, you will have followed the guidance of this book so will have already lost the fat you were previously carrying, hence you'll be ready to focus entirely on fuelling your bodies in the optimum fashion to sculpt yourself in to a Greek God. I'll be providing diet plans designed for both men and women, which undoubtedly will differ somewhat. We'll also investigate diets based on your natural body shape and lifestyle habits – remember my example of Scott being very tall, struggling to put weight on, and being on his feet all day. I'm the polar opposite. Even though we're training towards the same goal, our diets will most likely differ. As such I'll offer suitable examples for everyone else, to cater for such eventualities.

In addition, I will offer you the <u>complete</u> versions of my training programmes. If you've decided to follow my example and pick up those lovely weights, then by this stage you'll be familiar with bodybuilding, will have learned a few of the basics and will then be ready to follow me. We'll look at the training schedules, broken down into every single exercise. Then you'll have your four month programme ready for all the Vegas trips for the rest of your life…hmmm, not sure I'll still be going in my sixties but then never say never!

Once again, I'll offer a full breakdown for both the girls and the boys so everyone is fully catered for.

- Whilst the primary focus will be placed on my new diet and training regime, we're also going to spend some time with Luke – you'll remember my friend who spent six years in Asia as a healthy guy, only to return to England and become a great big fatty overnight. Luke won't be heading to the gym to hit the weights as that's not his cup of tea. It will therefore be my challenge to transform his body using the teachings of this book whilst introducing exercise to his routine in a completely different way. Look forward to Luke's results...

- You'll also recall I spoke of Mikey – who trained with me for a short while, then got fat and still hasn't managed to shift the weight. I spoke with Mikey and he's agreed to let me train him in preparation for his wedding. These days we live on opposite sides of the country so I'll have to train him remotely, which is the same model I'm following with you all. Look forward to seeing how Mikey does and make sure your before and after photos look better than his...

- I'll soon be looking for two further volunteers to follow my programme from this book, but under my direction. For this I'll meet with you and we'll build a plan together, I'll see you through to the end and we'll report the results in the second book. Anyone up to the challenge? Ideally I'd like to have both a man and a woman to work with.

- And finally, we'll have a section dedicated to celebrating the transformations of you, the wider reader. So don't forget to get in touch, and share your stories and photographs.

And so ladies and gents, that's it! Thanks for taking the time to work your way through this book and please do have complete faith in the instructions I've presented. Now it's down to you to apply them. Just stay focused, work hard and every time you find yourself slipping, take another hard look at that 'before' photo you've put on your fridge...and then drop and give me fifty! Let's close with a set of photos (what else!) For me it's easy, I simply look at these examples and immediately know which version of myself I want to be:

See you all at the pool in a few months xx